PRANKLOPEDIA

JULIE WINTERBOTTOM

ILLUSTRATED BY ROBB ALLEN

PRANKL

THE FUNNIEST, GROSSEST, CRAZIEST, NOT-MEAN PRANKS ON THE PLANET!

WORKMAN PUBLISHING
NEW YORK

OPEDIA

JULIE WINTERBOTTOM
ILLUSTRATED BY ROBB ALLEN

Library of Congress Cataloging-in-Publication Data is available.

ISBN 978-0-7611-8996-1

Design by Netta Rabin, Tae Won Yu and Phil Conigliaro
Cover design by Raquel Jaramillo

Workman books are available at special discounts when purchased in bulk for premiums and sales promotions as well as for fund-raising or educational use. Special editions or book excerpts can also be created to specification. For details, contact the Special Sales Director at the address below, or send an email to specialmarkets@workman.com.

Workman Publishing Co., Inc.
225 Varick Street
New York, NY 10014-4381

workman.com

Printed in China
First printing August 2016

10 9 8 7 6 5 4 3 2 1

PHOTO CREDITS: 6emeia.com: p.115 bottom left; BBC Photo Library: p.13; Benoit Lemoine/www.benoitlemoine.eu: p.115 middle left; Chad Nicholson: p.55; Fame: Barcrof p.115 middle left; fotolia: Aaron Amat p.143, amandarank001 p.30, anankkml p.35, Anyka p.223 2nd from top, berc p.142, brozova p.175 (composite), cheri131 p.69, dvarg p.161, Feydzhet Shabanov p.143 left, fotomaster p.221 (soup label insert), Georgios Kollidas p.8, Gordana Sermek p.223 top (composite), honzahruby p.167, Image Source IS2 p.93, jagodka p.47, mirovoi p.28, OlegD p.221 (soup label insert), olly p.175 composite, panoKreativ p.205 negative p.53, Popova Olga p.17, rangizzz p.143 right, Alexandr Steblovskiy p.69, Simone van den Berg p.223 top (composite), uwimages p.223 bottom, zabiamedve p.176, ZharAstudio p.92; Getty Images: Boston Globe p.31 bottom, Stuart Dee p.23, Luke Frazza/AFP p.126, Hulton Archive p.125 top, Hulton Archive/Stringer p.12, Elliot Neep p.9, George Skadding p.15, George Skaddling/Time Life Pictures p.125 middle, Chip Somodevilla p.127, Lane Stewart/Sports Illustrated p.144, Time Life Pictures p.125 bottom, Lawrence Thornton p.161, Joey Skaggs Archive: p.119; Mal Sharpe: p.41; © nialsmith.co.uk: p.77; Photofest: p.160; Reuters: Eloy Alonso p.129; Rex USA: Steve Alexander p.177 (Crop Circle), John Dee p.177, Eye Ubiquitous p.114; Edgar Mueller p.115 top, Courtesy of Kerry Scanlon, Kansas City, MO: p.79; Courtesy of Ravi Kochhar: p.31 top; Courtesy of Mark Jenkins/xmarkjenkinsx.com: p.115 bottom right; Courtesy of © Palace Administration Hellbrunn: p.67; Courtesy of Trevor Cox, University of Salford: p.59; Courtesy of Chris N. Brown: p.81, Courtesy of S.S. Adams LLC: p.73; Courtesy of LBJ Library/Yoichi Okamoto: p. 126, top; Public Domain: p.174.

acknowledgments

Thanks to the many people who helped make this book fun, funny, and good-looking:
Robb Allen, Brenda Bowen, Jordan and Finian Brown, Jim Chapin, Chris Duffy, Susan Hood,
Sue Macy, Marc Tyler Nobleman, Martha Pickerill, David Rappaport, Terri Watkins, Michele
Weisman, Dan Wetta, Sr., and the talented team at Workman Publishing: Raquel Jaramillo,
Krestyna Lypen, Netta Rabin, Tae Won Yu, Phil Conigliaro, Melissa Lucier, Beth Levy, Barbara
Peragine, and Robert Vargas. Thanks also to the Brooklyn Commune Laura Galen and everyone
at *Nick Mag* for their inspiration. And the people behind two excellent websites:
The Museum of Hoaxes and The Art of the Prank.

Special thanks to Susan Ferguson and the students and teachers at
Princeton Day School, Miriam Lewin, Steven Stern, and last but not least,
my partner-in-crime and long-suffering test subject, Stephen Wetta.

CONTENTS

The Pranks: A-Zzz

A Very Brief History
of PRANKING

NO ONE KNOWS WHO pulled the first prank, but chances are good it happened very early in human history. Some fun-loving cave guy probably greased the handle of his buddy's club with boar fat before they set out hunting one day. It seems the urge to fake out your fellow hominid is part of the human genetic code.

Luckily, some pranks from history actually got written down. One of the earliest recorded pranks happened almost 1,800 years ago, around A.D. 219. The story goes that the teenage Roman emperor Elagabalus placed special deflatable leather pillows around a low dining table for his most pompous guests. By the end of the meal, his victims were sitting on the floor. About 1,300 years later, an English monk named Thomas Betson fooled his fellow friars by putting a live beetle inside a hollowed-out apple, causing the fruit to rock back and forth by itself. Fast-forward to 1810, when an Englishman named Theodore Hook pulled off one of the craziest pranks ever. Hook made a bet with a friend that he could turn any home into the most talked-about address in London. Hook had nearly every product and service available in the City of London delivered over the course of a single day to the home of a Mrs. Tottenham. First thing in the morning, a load of coal arrived, followed by deliveries of furniture, musical instruments, flowers, bread, fish, a wedding cake, and much more. Doctors, dentists, gardeners, undertakers, even the mayor of London were all sent to the woman's house until there was a huge traffic jam on her street. Needless to say, he won the bet.

These are just a few highlights from the rich history of pranks. It's up to you to keep this ancient tradition alive. So get pranking! You'll be joining an elite club that includes Benjamin Franklin, Thomas Edison, President Franklin D. Roosevelt, Ellen DeGeneres, and George Clooney. If you get really good, you may even qualify someday for inclusion in this book's Prankster Hall of Fame!

CAUTION!

All the pranks contained herein have been tested on humans and they work. But naturally, you should exercise common sense and appropriate caution when doing them. The author and publisher are not responsible for any negative effects (including revenge pranks perpetrated on the user) that result from using this book.

FOUR THINGS TO KNOW ABOUT THIS BOOK

1 The pranks in this book are organized alphabetically, like encyclopedia entries. That means you can use the book to teach little siblings the alphabet when you're not busy pranking them.

2 Each prank in this book has a rating that tells you how much time and effort it takes:

DIFFICULTY LEVEL: **EASY**

DIFFICULTY LEVEL: **MEDIUM**

DIFFICULTY LEVEL: **EXPERT**

Quick and simple

A little more challenging

Experienced pranksters only!

3 You can do most of the pranks by yourself, but a few require help from an adult. Your adult should be more than happy to help out, because it means you won't be pulling the prank on them! These are marked with the sign shown at the right.

4 Most of the "Prankster Hall of Fame" entries described throughout the book are real. But a few are fakes. Can you spot them and avoid being the victim of a *Pranklopedia* prank?

HOW TO PULL THE PERFECT PRANK

1 PREPARE. Even very simple pranks work better if you think through what you are going to do before you approach your victim. For more complicated pranks, do a few test runs on a friend (or yourself) and adjust anything that isn't quite working.

2 TELL A GOOD STORY. It takes some acting skills to be an effective prankster (which might explain why Brad Pitt and George Clooney are so good at it). Make sure any story you invent sounds believable, and deliver it in your natural voice. If you suddenly start using a lot of fancy words or if you sound rehearsed, your victim will know something is up.

3 KEEP A STRAIGHT FACE. This gets easier with practice. Throw yourself into the story you are telling so that you practically believe it yourself, and don't think about the fact that you are about to prank your victim. If you still have trouble keeping a straight face, try this trick: Think about something serious before you get started (like the homework you're not doing because you are so busy pranking people). *Thinking* about serious things will help you *look* serious and make it that much easier to fool people.

4 SPREAD YOUR PRANKS OUT. If you do every prank in this book in one week, people won't fall for them—they'll just run when they see you coming!

PRANK RESPONSIBLY

Your pranks will go over much better (and you will also be much less likely to be grounded until the end of time) if you follow these rules:

1 **CHOOSE YOUR VICTIM CAREFULLY.** Someone who has a sense of humor and can't flunk you is a good general rule. Avoid school principals, police officers, or your mother on the day she has gotten a bad haircut and discovers the cat threw up all over the sofa.

2 **PRANKS SHOULD BE FUNNY, NOT MEAN.** It's fine to stick a sign on someone's back that says *High-Five Me!*, but don't write it in red paint that will ruin their favorite T-shirt. If your friend is deathly afraid of Jell-O, don't do any Jell-O pranks on him or her. (Try pudding pranks instead.)

3 **AVOID DAMAGE TO PROPERTY, PEOPLE, AND PETS.** That goes without saying, but we're saying it anyway.

4 **CLEAN UP ANY MESS.** Fake vomit is hilarious; the mess you left in the kitchen sink while making the fake vomit is not! Any prank that's particularly messy has this warning sign to the right.

BEWARE!
This prank may cause a mess. Be prepared to clean up!

WHEN GOOD PRANKS GO BAD

No matter how carefully you choose your victim, it's bound to happen once or twice: Instead of laughing, and perhaps congratulating you, your victim gets angry. This is usually a sign that the person has no sense of humor, but do not mention that! It's guaranteed to make things worse. Follow these tips instead:

1 If your victim doesn't realize that you are the perpetrator, you can:

⁕ Disappear for a while. Give your victim a chance to cool down—and hopefully forget the entire incident.

⁕ Make a copy of the form on the next page and leave it where your victim will find it. *Then* disappear for a while.

2 If you get caught red-handed, try a simple but flattering apology: "Aw, I was just joking. I picked you because you have such an awesome sense of humor!"

Happy pranking!

Greetings,

Were you recently the victim of a prank? Did you feel embarrassed, humiliated, angry, or just plain stupid? Did you suffer **damage to your property, clothing, reputation, or rear end?** If so, you are not alone. Thousands of innocent people get pranked every day by people who can find nothing better to do with their time. We know, because we have helped them. **And we can help *you*.**

Prank Victim's Revenge, Inc. helps you get back at the person who pranked you. Whether someone stuck a *High-Five Me!* sign on your back, short-sheeted your bed, or had a truckload of cow manure delivered to your house, **we will create the perfect revenge prank for your situation.** Our staff of retired lawyers and former circus performers will execute the payback prank for you, so you don't have to stoop to the level of your perpetrator.

Don't wait! The sooner you get revenge, the better you'll feel. And the perpetrator will quickly move on to other targets so you can return to your regular, boring life.

Call 1-555-PRNK to talk to an agent now! Ask about our **SPECIAL INTRODUCTORY RATE!** You get TWO customized revenge pranks and THREE prank phone calls to the target of your choice, PLUS a protective plastic coat, ALL for just $129.95! **REVENGE IS JUST A PHONE CALL AWAY**.

Very sincerely yours,

E. Z. Hokes

E. Z. Hokes

President and Chief Prank Officer
Prank Victim's Revenge, Inc.
66 Battery Park
Amityville, NY

the
pranks
A-Zzz

the prank

Morning is a great time for pulling pranks. People's defenses are down when they first wake up—that's a polite way of saying they're totally out of it. This prank is guaranteed to jolt your victim into a state of high alert. Try it on a sibling who is likely to leap out of bed before looking.

what you need

* Whipped cream (ready-made from a tub or can) or shaving cream
* A large piece of cardboard

what you do

THE SETUP

1 Observe your victim getting of bed in the morning. Notice where he steps first.

2 Put whipped cream or shaving cream on the piece of cardboard so it fills up most of the space.

PULL THE PRANK

1 Wait for your victim to fall sound asleep at night. Then sneak into his bedroom with the cream-covered cardboard.

2 Place the cardboard on the floor where he will step in the morning. Sneak back out.

3 Make sure you wake up the next morning before your victim so you can enjoy the reaction.

4 Rub "a little whipped cream in the wound" by innocently asking your victim if he was dancing on an ice-cream sundae in his sleep.

the prank

Imagine going down to the basement of your house at the start of the winter season to try on your ice skates to see if they still fit. You slide your foot into the right skate—and your toe hits something. You yank the skate off and peer inside. AHHHHHHHHHHHHHHHH! It's a dead mouse!

This prank was inspired by someone who really did find a furry surprise inside her skate. Her scream could be heard about 50 miles away. Fortunately, you don't need any actual dead rodents to do this prank—although a real-looking fake mouse from the pet store works nicely.

what you need

* Cotton balls, or a fake mouse (sold in the cat toy section of pet stores)

what you do

THE SETUP

1 Sneak into your victim's room when she is away or asleep.

2 Choose a pair of shoes you think she is likely to wear the next day. Stuff a handful of cotton balls, or a fake mouse in the toe of one or both shoes. Make sure you can't see the stuff when you're looking down at the shoe.

PULL THE PRANK

1 Wait for your victim to get dressed the next morning. If you used a fake mouse, you might want to wear some earplugs.

Extra, Extra!

Want to make your own fake mouse? You need two cotton balls, glue, string, tape, and a black marker. Use your fingers to gently stretch out each cotton ball so it's flatter and about 2 inches long. Glue the two pieces of cotton together to make the mouse's body. Gently pull the cotton on one end so it sticks out a little. Press it with your fingers to make a pointy nose. Cut a 3- to 4-inch piece of string. Use a tiny piece of tape to attach the string to the back of the mouse. Use the marker to make two eyes on the face, and your mouse is ready!

the prank

People who don't cover their nose when they sneeze are rude. But when *you* shower "snot" on the back of someone's neck, you are simply a good prankster. This prank is guaranteed to get a shriek. It works best on someone whose neck is exposed, so choose a victim who has short hair or their hair up in a ponytail.

what you need
* Water

what you do

THE SETUP

1 Make sure you pull this prank in a place where you have easy access to water. Do it in the kitchen when you are hanging out with friends. Or carry a water bottle with you so you can pull the prank when you're walking with your victim.

2 Look for an opportunity to get your hand close to the back of your victim's neck without drawing too much attention—when you are standing just behind the person or sitting side by side.

PULL THE PRANK

1 Casually mention that you have a really nasty cold. Cough, sniffle, and blow your nose a few times.

2 When you're ready to strike, dip your fingers into the water or pour a little water out of a bottle onto your hand. Then "sneeze" loudly as you flick the water onto the back of your victim's neck. Timing is important, so it's a good idea to practice this prank on a friend first to get it right.

Benjamin Franklin:

America's Founding Prankster

Benjamin Franklin is famous for helping to write the Declaration of Independence, inventing the lightning rod, and coming up with many other bright ideas. What most people don't know is that he was also a lifelong prankster. Franklin pulled one of his most successful hoaxes in 1722 when he was only 16. Pretending to be a middle-aged widow named Silence Dogood, he wrote a series of letters to a popular newspaper. He gave the widow's opinions on everything from religion to fashion. Readers loved the letters. In fact, a few men were so delighted with Widow Dogood that they sent her marriage proposals before young Ben revealed it was all a joke. Like Franklin's later pranks, this one had a social purpose: In the letters, Franklin poked fun at snobs and tried to make people think about how they treated others.

Benjamin Franklin

THE PRANKSTER HALL OF FAME

Animals Pull Pranks, Too!

Only humans pull pranks, right? Wrong! In 2009, a scientist named Dr. Sheila Getchew was studying hyenas at an animal preserve in East Africa when she observed something truly remarkable. Early one morning, Dr. Getchew was watching a group of hyenas resting outside their den. She noticed a young hyena leave the group and go inside the den. Soon it returned, carrying in its teeth a small plastic ziplock bag filled with air. It dropped the bag on the ground next to the other hyenas and sat nearby to watch. Moments later an older hyena trotted over to join the group. It sat down on the bag, without noticing it, and a loud farting sound shot out from his hindquarters as the air was forced out of the bag. The other hyenas immediately started howling hysterically and pointing at the older hyena, who covered its face with a paw, as if embarrassed.

Dr. Getchew realized she had just witnessed something no scientist had ever seen before: a wild animal pranking another animal. She theorized that the young hyena had found the plastic bag in a trashcan on the preserve and somehow managed to inflate it.

In 2010, Dr. Getchew published her observations in the *Journal of Hyena Studies*. Her article, "Practical Jokes in the Hyena Population of East Africa," is still talked about among zoologists. You can find it in the book *Scientific Hogwash: Questionable "Discoveries" in Science.*

A wild hyena laughs at a prank.

the prank

Ah, the fool's errand. This classic prank has been around for hundreds of years. (See April Fools' Day on page 12.) It's simple to execute, and the variations are limitless. All you need is a sibling or friend gullible enough to ask for absurd—and nonexistent—products the next time you're at the store. You can have him or her look for these one at a time. Or, you can give someone a list. Make sure to include real items on the list so they don't get suspicious.

what you need

* A list of mostly real items with a few ridiculous, nonexistent ones

what you do

THE SETUP

1 Invent a few weird but real-sounding items for your victim to ask for at a store.

Here are some examples to get you started:

PULL THE PRANK

1 Next time you're in a store with a sibling or a friend, tell the person to ask a store employee for one of your ridiculous fake products or hand them a list with mostly real items and a few fake ones. Hang out nearby so you can enjoy the conversation.

* non-sticky glue
* peeled grapes
* dissolving tea
* a knee-sharpener
* noncarbonated soda
* self-tying shoelaces
* dried raisins
* -2% milk
* 8-inch marshmallows
* eyelash repair kit
* 3-D paint
* elbow grease
* bacon stretcher
* ice softener
* shoe silencer

April Fools' Day

April 1 is the one day of the year when people are actually *expected* to pull pranks. Even the most boring, humorless grown-up will switch the salt and the sugar or move all the clocks ahead by an hour. Why April 1? No one knows for sure how the tradition got going. Some say it started in 1563 in France, when the government decided to switch to a new calendar and move the start of the year from Easter to January 1. The story goes that people living in the countryside didn't hear about the switch and continued to celebrate New Year's Day in early April. They were called April Fools and had tricks played on them. It's a good story, but it's probably not true.

Eighteenth-century pranksters carry on an ancient tradition.

More likely, April Fools' Day grew out of an ancient tradition of celebrating the arrival of spring with silliness and hijinks. For centuries, people in India have flung brightly colored powders at each other during a spring festival called *Holi*. The ancient Romans used to let loose during a festival called *Hilaria* on March 25. Later, during the Middle Ages, people in Europe dressed in disguises and played tricks on each other during *Festum Fatuorum* (Festival of Fools).

Whatever its origins, April Fools' Day caught hold in Europe and America, especially during the 1700s. That's when the first KICK ME sign got stuck on some poor soul's back. It's also when a prank known as a "fool's errand" got its start in England. A practical joker would send a child to the store for "pigeon's milk" or "striped paint" or another nonexistent item. (See the April Fool's Errand prank on page 10.) In more recent decades, people have pulled off some of the wildest pranks ever on April 1. In 1974 a man named Oliver "Porky" Bickar convinced residents of Sitka, Alaska, that a long-inactive volcano near their town had suddenly blown. Bickar had tossed hundreds of old tires into the cone of the dormant volcano and set them on fire. (Bickar warned the police ahead of time about the prank so no one got hurt. Still, this is a good example of a prank you should not try at home—or anywhere else.)

Many newspapers, radio stations, and websites love to fool their audiences on April 1. One of the funniest media hoaxes in modern history took place on April 1, 1957—long before *The Onion* and *The Daily Show* made fake news a part of daily life. A British TV news show reported that due to an unusually warm winter, the spaghetti harvest in Switzerland had started early. *Spaghetti* harvest? That's right. The report showed a video

A spaghetti picker hard at work.

of a farm family in Switzerland pulling pasta from trees. The narrator explained how the spaghetti weevil, an insect that had once destroyed the spaghetti harvest, had been defeated. In 1957 many people in Britain had never tasted pasta, so they didn't question the report. Instead, hundreds of viewers jammed the phone lines of the TV station with serious questions about the harvest. Some wanted to know where they could get a spaghetti plant of their own!

Every day is April 1 to me!

the prank

When you hear the words "opera singer," you probably don't think "brilliant prankster." But the inspiration for this prank will make you think again! Many years ago, one opera singer decided to punk another during a performance. The victim had to sing onstage while holding a muff—a tube-shaped piece of fur that women and girls used to carry to keep their hands warm. As she sang, the victim stuck her hands in the muff—and suddenly started reeling around the stage, flapping her arms. The prankster had placed a piece of mushy, overripe banana inside the muff. When the victim touched it, she was horrified! Fortunately, you do not need a muff or an opera singer to pull this prank—just an old banana and a friend who likes to show off his biceps.

what you need

* A piece of mushy, gooey, overripe banana

what you do

THE SETUP

1. Put the piece of banana in the palm of your hand.

2. Cup your hand a little so the stuff stays put—and out of sight.

PULL THE PRANK

1. Challenge your friend to an arm-wrestling contest. When he clasps your hand, he'll have a gooey surprise waiting for him! An added bonus: You will very likely win the contest!

Art Pranks

For many people, art is serious business—certainly not the place for pranks. But some artists like to combine making art with making mischief. Here are three artfully artful capers.

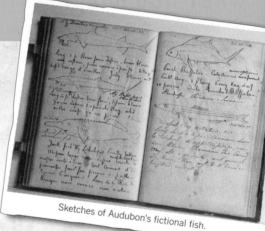

Sketches of Audubon's fictional fish.

FUN WITH FISH

During the late 1700s and early 1800s, there was a mad rush among amateur scientists to discover and name new species of plants and animals. A naturalist named Constantine Rafinesque eagerly joined the search. While he accurately named about 30 new species, he sometimes went a little overboard: He would write about new creatures based on very little evidence. If he read about an exotic animal in a travel book, for instance, he would give it a scientific name and describe it as if it were fact. Rafinesque's sometimes sloppy science made him an easy mark for a prank by the famous wildlife painter John James Audubon.

In 1818 Audubon made drawings of about a dozen fictional fish species, including one he called the devil-jack diamond fish. He described it as having hard, bulletproof scales that a woodsman could use with a piece of flint to start a fire. Rafinesque swallowed Audubon's story hook, line, and sinker. He gave the "new" fish the Latin name *Litholepis adamantinus*, which means "unbreakable stone scales," and published it along with Audubon's other made-up fish as new species.

ART THEFT IN REVERSE

Museums go to great lengths to make sure no one steals paintings off their walls, but no one usually worries about people putting paintings *on* the walls. No doubt that made it easier for the British graffiti artist known as Banksy to pull a series of heists in reverse.

In 2005 Banksy walked into four major museums in New York City and quietly hung his own paintings on the walls, without anyone noticing. One painting stayed up for six days before workers realized it didn't belong to the museum. Later that year, Banksy hung a fake "prehistoric" cave painting in the world-renowned British Museum in London. The painting showed a cave person hunting while pushing a shopping cart. Bansky included a caption that read: "Early man venturing towards the out-of-town hunting grounds." A couple of days passed before museum workers discovered the prank. They seemed to have a good sense of humor about it, though: They decided to keep the painting in their permanent collection—something many artists would kill for!

EAR THIS!

In 1935 the Museum of Modern Art in New York City hosted a rare exhibit of Vincent van Gogh's paintings. Thousands of people flocked to the museum. Some wanted to see the art. But many who went were more interested in the shocking story that van Gogh had cut off part of his ear—at least that's what illustrator and prankster Hugh Troy believed. Troy was irritated that the crowds kept him and other art lovers from getting a good look at the art. He reportedly devised a devilish prank to solve the problem. He created a fake ear out of dried beef. He placed it in a velvet-lined display box and left it on a table in the exhibit, with an official-looking sign explaining that it was the actual ear that van Gogh had lobbed off. Soon the crowds were gathered around the fake ear, and Troy could finally see the paintings. There is some debate about whether or not Troy actually got his "ear" into the museum—but the story has entered pranklore, perhaps for its sheer genius. (You can read more about prankster Hugh Troy on page 35.)

Vincent van Gogh

DIFFICULTY LEVEL: MEDIUM

MR. MINT, MEET MR. GARLIC.

HEY, WANT A MINT?

SURE, THANKS!

YUCK!!

SEE YA!

the prank

Most people start gobbling mints or chugging mouthwash at the slightest hint that they have bad breath. But a malodorous mouth can be a good thing—when you want people to leave you alone, for instance. Convince your friends and family that there is a brand-new breath mint designed to *give* you bad breath and drive bothersome people away.

what you need

ADULT HELP

* A roll of mints (Life Savers or similar brand)
* Fresh garlic
* "Repel Mints" label on page 211
* Scissors
* Tape or glue

what you do

THE SETUP

1 Remove the paper label from the roll of mints. Open one end of the foil wrapper and take out two mints. Put one mint aside for later while you . . .

2 . . . add garlic flavor to the other. Here's how: **Ask an adult** to help you peel one clove of the garlic and slice it in half. Rub the juicy side all over the mint. Put the mint on a plate to dry (about 10 minutes), and wash the garlic off your hands.

3 Put the garlic-coated mint back in the pack and close the foil.

4 Carefully cut out the prank label for "Repel Mints" on page 211. Wrap the label around the roll of mints and tape or glue it closed. Make sure you know which end has the garlic mint.

PULL THE PRANK

1 Put the mint you set aside in your mouth and walk up to your victim holding the pack of Repel Mints. Open the end with the garlic mint and say, "Want a mint?" Since most people can't say no to free candy, your victim will probably take the mint and pop it in his mouth. If not, you may need to do a little cajoling: "You sure? They're really delicious."

2 Wait a few seconds for the garlic taste to hit. Your victim will probably say something like, "Yuck. What's in these?" At this point, show him the label and cheerfully explain: "It's a new kind of mint called 'Repel Mints.' They give you bad breath to make irritating people go away. See ya!" Then make a fast exit.

BANANA MAGIC

DIFFICULTY LEVEL: *EXPERT*

THE TOOL!

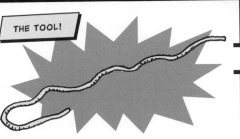

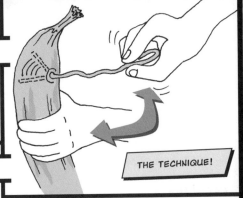

THE TECHNIQUE!

THE OUTCOME!

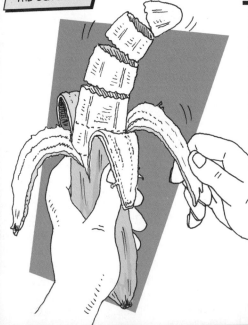

THE REACTION!

I WONDER IF IT'S ONE OF THOSE GENETICALLY MODIFIED BANANAS!

the prank

Bananas are a nearly perfect food. They taste good, they're good for you, and they come with their own nifty packaging. The only thing that could make them better would be if they were presliced. That's where this prank comes in! With a little practice, you can slice a banana into neat rounds without ever peeling it. When you give it to a friend to peel, they'll go totally bananas as the fruit magically falls apart into bite-size pieces! This prank is perfect for the school lunchroom, but practice it at home first until you get it right.

what you need

* A large paper clip
* Dishwashing soap
* A banana that's ripe, but not brown

what you do

THE SETUP

1 Unbend the paper clip and straighten out the kinks. Wash it with dishwashing soap, rinse, and dry. You'll use this thin metal stick to slice the banana from the inside.

2 Carefully poke a hole in the banana skin about a half-inch from one end. Push the paper clip straight through the flesh until it touches the skin on the other side, but don't let it poke through the other side of the banana.

3 Now swivel the paper clip back and forth inside the banana. This is the part that takes some practice. Keep the paper clip straight and just graze the inside surface of the peel with the tip. You want to slice off the end of the banana without piercing the skin.

4 Repeat step 3 every half inch along the banana until you have sliced the whole fruit. There will be a line of dots where you

stuck the paper clip in, but the dots should be small and barely noticeable.

5 Now test out the banana by peeling it. If you did your cutting correctly, it should fall apart into half-inch slices. If it doesn't, check to see if you sliced all the way through the flesh. Try again until you master the process.

PULL THE PRANK

1 If you plan to do this prank in the school lunchroom, prepare the banana in the morning just before you leave the house so it doesn't turn brown where you poked holes in it.

2 Whether you do it at school or at home, here's a good setup: Hand the trick banana to your victim and say, "I can't seem to get the peel started on this. Can you peel it for me?" When the banana falls apart in pieces, act really surprised. Say something like, "Wow, I wonder if this is one of those genetically modified bananas!"

DIFFICULTY LEVEL: EASY

THAT NIGHT, BEFORE THEIR PARENTS' DINNER PARTY...

IT'S PRANKING TIME!

YEAH!

WHERE'S THE OUT HOUSE?

I KNEW I SHOULD HAVE GONE BEFORE I LEFT THE HOUSE!

RESTROOM CLOSED FOR MAINTENANCE

PLEASE USE THE OUTDOOR FACILITIES UNTIL FURTHER NOTICE

OBJECTS IN MIRROR ARE WEIRDER THAN THEY APPEAR!

WELL JEEPERS! FLUSH ALREADY!!

THIS TOILET IS VOICE-ACTIVATED SAY FLUSH TOILET IN A LOUD, CLEAR VOICE WHEN YOU ARE DONE USING IT.

the prank

Bathrooms are a good place for posting prank signs because you're pretty much guaranteed a captive audience. Display these signs and put some comedy in the commode! A good time to pull this prank is during one of your parents' fanciest dinner parties.

what you need

* Bathroom signs on pages 187–189
* Scissors
* Tape

what you do

THE SETUP

1. Carefully cut out the signs on pages 187–189.

2. Tape each sign in the appropriate place in the bathroom.

PULL THE PRANK

1. Be prepared to offer assistance to anyone who can't find the outdoor facilities or needs help activating the flush mechanism.

VERY IMPORTANT PRANKS
V.I.P.

Watch Where You Flush

Like many successful inventors, Apple Computer cofounder Steve Wozniak flies on planes a lot. He also happens to love practical jokes. He once brought a little humor onboard a plane when he placed official-looking foil labels on the doors of the toilets that said "Do Not Flush Over Cities."

"Is it safe to flush?"

the prank

Special delivery! This prank is perfect for the person in your family who is always shopping online for clothes, gadgets, or anything else that comes in a box. It requires a little planning: When your victim gets a package in the mail, save the box. Wait a few weeks and then use the box to pull this prank.

ADULT HELP

what you need

* An empty cardboard box addressed to your victim
* Scissors
* A large bag of popcorn or plenty of packing peanuts (the bits of Styrofoam-like stuff that are used to pack and protect breakable objects)
* Clear packing tape

what you do

THE SETUP

1 **Ask an adult** to help you cut out the bottom panel of the box. Make sure the sides look normal.

2 When your victim is not around, place the box right side up on a table or counter where your victim is used to finding packages that have just arrived in the mail. Open the top and fill the box just to the top with popcorn or packing peanuts.

3 Carefully tape the top of the box shut, so it looks like a new package that's just arrived. The box should look completely normal.

PULL THE PRANK

1 Wait for your victim to walk in and see the box, or yell to him that he got a package in the mail.

2 When the person picks up the trick box, the popcorn or packing peanuts will spill all over. This is a good time to exit, so you don't have to clean up the mess. (Actually, you'll probably end up pushing a broom, but it's worth a try!)

the prank

Because your parents are unlikely to loosen up and let you drive anytime soon, you'll have to find other ways to make being in a car more interesting. Try posting these prank signs—or make your own signs—and bring some hilarity to the highway on your next long family trip or a short drive to the store.

what you need

* Car signs on pages 191–203
* Scissors
* Tape (optional)

what you do

THE SETUP

1 Carefully cut out the signs on pages 191–203.

2 Hold one of the signs to the window when your family's car is stuck in traffic or waiting at a red light. Or tape a sign to the rear bumper if it's not raining.

PULL THE PRANK

1 Sit back and enjoy your fellow travelers' reactions.

VERY IMPORTANT PRANKS

V.I.P.

School Traffic Jam

In 2006, 94 high school students in Austin, Minnesota, pulled an ingenious traffic-stopping prank. A busy street separates two buildings on their school's campus. An underground tunnel also connects the buildings. At an appointed time, the students began crossing the street and then circling back through the underground tunnel and crossing the street again, so that the crosswalk was constantly filled with a stream of pedestrians (including one dressed as a cow and another as a chicken). Traffic was tied up for nearly ten minutes as cars lined up, waiting for the seemingly endless parade to . . . well, um . . . end.

CHIPS, AHA!

the prank

Do you have a friend who always reaches for your just-opened bag of chips without asking? That person might refuse all snack offers after sticking a hand in *this* bag of tricks.

what you need

* A snack-size bag of chips
* A can or tub of whipped cream
* A spoon

what you do

THE SETUP

1 Open the bag of chips and empty it into a bowl. Use the spoon to fill the bag about two-thirds full with whipped cream from a tub, or use a spray can to fill it partway. Be careful not to get whipped cream near the opening, where your victim might see it.

2 Take a few chips out of the bowl and hide the rest.

PULL THE PRANK

1 Approach your victim, holding a few chips in one hand and the bag in the other. While chomping on a chip, say, "Want some?" and offer the bag. Hold the bag so it's difficult to see inside. Your victim will jump when her hand touches the cool, moist cream instead of a crispy chip.

2 If you want to freak her out even more, try innocently asking, "Oh, no, did something die in there?"

College Pranks

If **your parents** haven't already given you enough reasons for going to college, here's a new one: College students have pulled some of the most inspired, ambitious pranks ever. Here are just a few that deserve an A+.

CARD TRICK

As far as we know, you can't actually major in pranks at college. But if you go to the California Institute of Technology, you can come close. The school is famous for perfectly engineered pranks—which might have something to do with the fact that many students go there to study engineering. The Rose Bowl Hoax is a shining example of the students' technical wizardry.

The Rose Bowl is a football tournament that is held every year in Pasadena, right down the road from the Caltech campus. Caltech's team is never good enough to play in the tournament, but in 1961 a group of students hatched an idea for a prank that would finally put Caltech in the game. One of the competing teams, the Washington Huskies, was planning a series of card stunts at halftime. Everyone in the stadium would be given a colored card to hold up. Together, the cards would spell out different messages when seen from afar—or on television. A Caltech student managed to find out where the Huskies' head cheerleader kept the master plan for the cards. While the Huskies were busy visiting Disneyland the day before the big game, Caltech got the master plan and replaced it with a new version.

The next day at halftime, the Huskies fans started doing the card stunts as a national TV audience watched. The first 11 stunts were fine. Then the insanity began: The 12th stunt was supposed to be Washington's mascot, a husky. Instead, it was a beaver, the mascot of Caltech. Stunt 13 was supposed to spell out HUSKIES, but it read backward: SEIKSUH. The final stunt was the real winner: In gigantic letters that filled the stadium, the Huskies fans unwittingly spelled out one word: CALTECH.

Visitors gather to see the sunken lady up close.

LADY LIBERTY TAKES A SOAKING

During the winter of 1979, two students at the University of Wisconsin, Madison, made good on a crazy promise. Jim Mallon and Leon Varjian had announced that they would move the Statue of Liberty from New York City to Wisconsin if they got elected to student government. No one took them seriously until . . . one day in February, rising up out of a huge frozen lake near the campus was Lady Liberty herself. Her gigantic green head and torch-bearing hand rose high above the icy surface. Mallon and Varjian told people they'd had the statue flown in by helicopter but the cable holding it broke and Lady Liberty crashed through the ice. The real story? The pranksters had the statue built from wire, papier-mâché, and plywood and then hauled it to the lake.

A TOUGH PARKING SPOT

Another school that is famous for producing engineers—and pranks—is the Massachusetts Institute of Technology (MIT for short). In 1994 a group of students managed to park a campus police car on top of a huge building known as the Great Dome. Getting a car onto the roof of any building is hard. But the Dome is 15 stories high, and the only way to get to the roof was through a small trapdoor that was always locked. How did the students do it? Instead of trying to move the whole car, they took it apart. Then they pulled pieces of the body up the side of the building using a system of rollers. It took them three tries before they succeeded. Once they got all the pieces to the top, they reassembled the car so it looked normal. They even made the lights on the roof flash and placed a dummy police officer in the driver's seat. The finishing touch was a parking ticket on the windshield, because, of course, the car was in a no-parking zone.

The next day, news teams swarmed in and the hoax became one of the most famous college pranks of all time. A side note: The MIT pranksters were not the first to place a car on the roof of a building. In 1958 three students of engineering (what else?) at Cambridge University in England hauled an engineless van to the top of their Senate Building, all in one piece!

A parking spot with a view!

the prank

Even people who never lose their cool tend to freak out when their computer freezes. The thought of losing all that data—or not being able to play another round of Plants vs. Zombies—is just too awful. You can fool your parents or siblings into thinking the family computer is on the fritz without doing any real harm to the computer (although you may do temporary harm to your relationship). It takes some time to set up the prank, but the meltdown you get to witness will be memorable. Of course, keep in mind that it's generally not a good idea to mess with someone else's computer. Use your judgment, and when in doubt, check with an adult.

what you need

✱ Access to a family member's computer

what you do

THE SETUP

If you have a Mac . . .

1 Take a screenshot of the desktop by holding "Command" and "Shift" and then hitting "3."

2 This picture file should have been saved to your desktop.

3 Double-click on the picture you just took to open it.

4 Make the image take up the full screen by holding "Command" and "Shift" and then hitting "F." If you're not ready to pull the prank yet and need to exit full-screen mode, move the cursor and hit the "x" that appears at the bottom of the screen or hit the "Esc" (escape) button on your keyboard.

If you have a PC . . .

1 Take a screenshot of the desktop by using the "Prt Scr" (Print Screen) button on your keyboard.

2 Paste this picture into a picture-editing program, such as Paint. Save this image to your desktop.

3 Create a new folder on the desktop. Move the screenshot into this folder.

4 Double-click on the folder to open it. Then right-click on the picture,

continues ➥

hover over "Open With," and select "Windows Photo Viewer."

5 Make the image take up the full screen by either hitting the center button in the taskbar at the bottom of Windows Photo Viewer or by hitting "F11" on your keyboard. If you're not ready to pull the prank yet and need to exit full-screen mode, hit the "Esc" (Escape) button on your keyboard.

FOR MORE COMPUTER PRANKS, GO TO WORKMAN.COM/COMPUTERPRANKS

PULL THE PRANK

1 Now your victim's computer should *look* normal, but because the icons and the taskbar are just part of the screenshot you took, they won't open or move or do anything they're supposed to do. It will appear as if the computer is totally frozen.

2 Make sure you are nearby the next time your victim uses his computer so you can witness the panic. Or speed things along and ask him to look something up for you. You might want to take pity on your victim and show him how to exit full-screen mode before he calls the help desk!

Hugh Troy:
The Human Rhino

Hugh Troy was an artist who illustrated children's books. He also excelled at the art of pranking. He is perhaps best known for a hoax he reportedly played when he was a student at Cornell University in the 1920s. As Troy told it, he knew a certain professor who had a wastebasket that was made out of a rhinoceros' foot. One day after a big snowstorm, Troy and a friend borrowed the wastebasket and used it to make a trail of rhino footprints across the snow. When they got to the edge of a frozen lake, they cut a big hole in the ice so it looked like the rhino had fallen in. When the story that a rhino had drowned in the lake spread through the town, some people stopped drinking the tap water—until Troy revealed that he was the rascal behind the rhino. There is some debate about whether Troy actually executed all of the pranks he is known for. There is no doubt, however, that he was a genius at dreaming up one-of-a-kind capers.

Troy had some good advice on how to invent your own pranks. He said that rather than consciously trying to think up a prank, you should just be open to ideas that come to you as you observe what's around you.

the prank

As a rule, you shouldn't mess with someone else's computer. But this computer mouse prank is harmless and quick—sort of like a real mouse. Try it on an especially technologically challenged adult.

what you need

* Access to a friend's or family member's computer mouse (it must be an optical or laser mouse, the kind with a red light)
* A small square of paper
* Tape

what you do

THE SETUP

1 When your victim is away from his computer, attach the small square of paper to the bottom of the mouse with tape so it covers the little light.

2 Make sure the paper doesn't stick out along the edges of the mouse. Tear off the edges if necessary.

PULL THE PRANK

1 Turn the mouse upright and leave it where you found it. When your victim tries to use the mouse, it will appear to be "dead." You can offer to make funeral arrangements, but if it looks like the person is about to purchase a new mouse, it's time to 'fess up.

FOR MORE COMPUTER PRANKS, GO TO WORKMAN.COM/COMPUTERPRANKS

VERY IMPORTANT PRANKS

V.I.P.

A Giggle from Google

Every year on April Fools' Day, technology companies (such as Google) try to outdo each other with their online pranks. In 2011 some computer wizards at a college in California outdid Google at its own prank.

On April 1 Google told users of Gmail that it was introducing a new version of the service called Google Motion that let them control Gmail with their bodies. The company produced a video that showed how the service worked: Users could swing one arm backward to reply to a message; swing two arms to reply to all; and lick their hand and tap their knee to send a message. It was all supposed to be a joke. But the joke was on Google when researchers at the University of Southern California quickly created a version of Google Motion that really worked! Hours after Google announced its prank version of Google Motion, the researchers posted a video showing their real version. They introduced it by saying, "For whatever reason, Google's application doesn't appear to work. So we demonstrate our solution." Game over!

the prank

Your family and friends probably love you, but does that love extend to a desire to see your face every time their computer goes to sleep? You'll soon find out! (Remember, as a rule you shouldn't meddle with someone else's computer, so check with an adult if you have doubts.)

what you need

* Access to a sibling's or friend's computer
* A silly picture of yourself

what you do

THE SETUP

1 Take a picture of yourself doing something ridiculous. Here are a few suggestions to get you started:

* A close-up headshot of you sticking your tongue out at the camera with an open banana peel or pair of underpants on your head.
* You looking terrified and pretending to have a stuffed animal stuck on your neck, as if the thing is attacking you.
* You looking very serious while pretending to read a very serious book that is very seriously upside down.

2 Save the picture to your computer and email it to yourself so you'll have easy access to it when you're ready to pull this prank.

3 You will follow different directions depending on whether your victim has a Mac or a PC.

If your victim has a Mac . . .

1 Download and save your photo, or photos, in a separate folder or event in iPhoto.

2 Go to the Apple menu and select "System Preferences."

3 Select the "View" menu and then "Desktop & Screen Saver."

4 Select iPhoto and then the folder that contains the photo, or photos, you want to use.

5 Make sure the computer is set to go to sleep after a short interval.

If your victim has a PC . . .

1 Download and save your photo, or photos, in a separate folder in My Pictures.

continues

COMPUTER SCREEN SAVER INSANITY (continued)

2 Right-click on the desktop and select "Personalize."

3 Click on "Screen Saver."

4 Select "Photos" from the drop-down menu. Then select "Settings" and then "Browse" to choose which photo, or photos, you want to use. Hit "Save" and then click "OK."

5 Make sure the computer is set to go to sleep after a short interval.

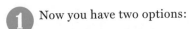

FOR MORE COMPUTER PRANKS, GO TO
WORKMAN.COM/COMPUTERPRANKS

PULL THE PRANK

1 Now you have two options:

❋ You can wait for your victim to let her computer fall asleep—you'll know when she's discovered your special present when you get the call/text/email asking why your lovely face is all over her screen.

❋ You can also speed up the process—and enjoy the reaction in person—if you ask to use your friend's computer after you've set the prank in motion and the computer is asleep. Tell your friend you want to show her something so she'll be looking at the screen when you wake the computer up.

She might never trust you with her computer again, but hopefully her reaction will make up for that.

Coyle & Sharpe:

IS Your Head a Sugar Bowl?

Long before reality TV was invented, two radio hosts from San Francisco were walking up to strangers in the street, asking them ridiculous questions, and recording the results with a hidden microphone. Dressed in suits and sounding very serious, Jim Coyle and Mal Sharpe asked their victims questions like, "Would you let someone use your head as a sugar bowl?" Or, "Would you be willing to help future generations of humans fly by having chicken wings attached to your forehead?" Amazingly, people gave serious answers, which were then broadcast on Coyle and Sharpe's nightly radio show to hilarious effect. Coyle once said their secret was in "pushing their victims as far as they'll go before they take a poke at us." During the 1960s the duo duped thousands of people—without getting poked—and entertained millions of listeners at home.

Mal Sharpe and Jim Coyle

DIFFICULTY LEVEL: MEDIUM

PUT SOME FLOUR IN YOUR HAND.

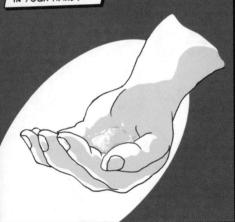

PRACTICE TO GET IT RIGHT!

COUGH

I WAS HELPING MY MOM BAKE COOKIES EARLIER...

AAAHHH!

the prank

BEWARE!
This prank may cause a mess. Be prepared to clean Up!

Using just a spoonful of flour and your supurb storytelling skills, you can completely freak out your friends. Tell them you were helping your mom bake cookies earlier, or you were doing a science experiment, and—*cough cough*—something went wrong.

what you need

* A teaspoon of flour

what you do

THE SETUP

1 Practice this prank alone before you try it on your victim. Place the spoonful of flour in the palm of one hand. Make a loose fist with that hand, the way you do when you cough. It's important not to squeeze your fist too tightly. And remember not to breathe in the flour when you lift your fist to your mouth!

2 Now try coughing into your fist. Your cough should force the flour out of the opening at the other end of your fist where your pinkie is. You'll need to try tightening or loosening your fist until you can make it work just right.

PULL THE PRANK

1 With flour in one hand, walk up to your victim and start a conversation. Hold your hand down by your side so it looks perfectly normal. In the middle of the conversation, when you have your victim's full attention, bring your fist up to your mouth and start coughing. Your victim will be shocked to see you coughing up clouds of white stuff.

2 At this point, you have two choices: You can say absolutely nothing, and act like it's perfectly normal to cough up white stuff. Or you can freak out, too. Say, "Man, that feels better! I was having trouble breathing. I had to clear my lungs."

Prank #16

DIFFICULTY LEVEL: MEDIUM

the prank

Most people think it's their lucky day when they find a dollar bill lying on the sidewalk. But when your victims reach for this trick bill, they'll wish they had kept walking. The dollar seems to move under its own power—but it's really you, at the other end of a piece of fishing line.

what you need

* Clear (not colored) fishing line (sold at sporting goods stores)
* Scissors
* A dollar bill
* Tape

what you do

THE SETUP

1 Cut a piece of fishing line about 8 feet long.

2 Tape one end of the fishing line to the back of the dollar bill.

3 Find a good place to pull the prank. A sidewalk where you can hide behind some bushes or a fence is good, or a hallway where you can hide around a corner or in a doorway.

PULL THE PRANK

1 Place the dollar bill where people will walk by, then grab the other end of the line and go to your hiding place.

2 When someone reaches for the dollar, yank it away just before they touch it. If you yank just a little, you can get them to grab for it again before they realize they've taken your bait.

VERY IMPORTANT PRANKS

V.I.P.

The Driverless Car

More than 50 years ago, a creative young man named Quent Beecham reportedly rigged his family's car so that it appeared to operate without a driver. Beecham was actually driving from the backseat. He attached reins to the steering wheel and used a long pole with a loop of wire on the end to work the gears. People in Yonkers, New York, where Beecham lived, were shocked to see the car pass by with no one at the wheel. Needless to say, this prank falls into the "Do Not Try This at Home" (or anywhere else, for that matter) category.

An amazingly fake self-driving car.

the prank

Watch your parents' mood instantly darken when they arrive home to find one of these "official notices" hanging from the doorknob.

what you need

* A doorknob hanger on pages 215–217
* Scissors

what you do

THE SETUP

1 Cut out the doorknob hangers on pages 215–217. Then carefully cut out the center circle (the part you'll slip over the doorknob).

2 Choose which doorknob hanger you want to use and slip the hanger on the front doorknob when no one is watching.

PULL THE PRANK

1 Wait for the reactions when your parents find the hanger and read the bad news: When they start fuming, say something sympathetic like, "I'm all for recycling, but this is totally insane!" or, "What?! We can't use the toilet for an entire day?!"

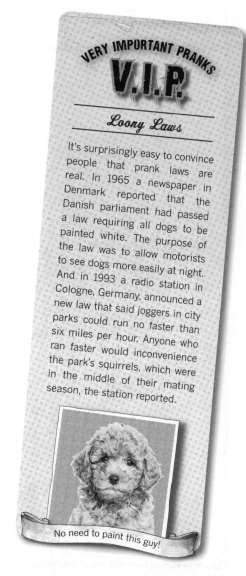

VERY IMPORTANT PRANKS
V.I.P.

Loony Laws

It's surprisingly easy to convince people that prank laws are real. In 1965 a newspaper in Denmark reported that the Danish parliament had passed a law requiring all dogs to be painted white. The purpose of the law was to allow motorists to see dogs more easily at night. And in 1993 a radio station in Cologne, Germany, announced a new law that said joggers in city parks could run no faster than six miles per hour. Anyone who ran faster would inconvenience the park's squirrels, which were in the middle of their mating season, the station reported.

No need to paint this guy!

the prank

By age five, most people have figured out how to drink a soda without spilling it all over themselves. You can undo all that progress by making a simple adjustment to your victim's soda can. It's best to use a can of seltzer or club soda or a clear, nonsugary soda for this prank. Otherwise, you might end up having to pay your victim's dry-cleaning bill.

what you need

* 2 cans of seltzer
* 1 pushpin

what you do

THE SETUP

1 Use the pushpin to poke a tiny hole in the side of one can about three-quarters of an inch from the top, on the side where the tab opens.

PULL THE PRANK

1 Offer your victim a drink, and then hand him the trick can to open. Sip calmly from your own can and try not to crack up when your victim dribbles soda all over himself.

2 You can bolster your innocence and pester your victim by offering a napkin and saying, "Wow, you sure are making a mess! Do you need a sippy cup?"

VERY IMPORTANT PRANKS

V.I.P.

The Drink That Helps You Think

In 2005, Google announced a new drink called Google Gulp. It said the drink would make people better at searching the Internet by upping their intelligence. The website explained how the miracle beverage worked: The lip of the bottle contained a special scanner that instantly analyzed a person's DNA or genetic code. A feature called "Auto Drink" delivered a customized mix of chemicals to the brain that made the organ work better and faster. Sound too good to be true? It was. Google Gulp was introduced on April 1 and was one of Google's annual April Fools' jokes. The fake product didn't quench anyone's thirst for knowledge, but it did satisfy the minimum daily requirement of pranks!

EW! BIRD TURD

WANT TO MAKE SOME BIRD POOP?

TWO DAYS LATER...

IT'S DRY! NOW TO FIND DAD'S HAT...

BIRD POOP CHART

eagle | sparrow | HAWK | FALCON

DAD, I FOUND YOUR HAT ON THE DECK. WHAT'S THAT WHITE STUFF ON IT?

OH, NO!

HA!

the prank

This fake bird poop looks just like the real thing. Make sure you wait for it to dry completely so it won't make a stain. Then leave it on someone's hat or jacket or on your parents' car windshield and watch their feathers get ruffled.

what you need

* White puff paint (sold at craft stores)
* White glue (Elmer's or a similar brand)
* Disposable plastic cup or bowl
* Plastic spoon
* Waxed paper
* Salt
* Pepper

EW! WARNING

This prank is pretty gross, so choose your victim wisely. Pick someone who laughs hysterically at fart jokes and other bathroom humor—not the crank who gives you a withering look of disgust.

what you do

THE SETUP

1 Mix equal parts of puff paint and glue together in the cup or bowl.

2 Pour a drop of the paint/glue mixture onto a piece of waxed paper. Try to get the shape of a bird dropping. If your victim is extremely gullible, you can make a very large bird dropping.

3 Take a pinch of salt in your fingers and scatter just a few grains on the paint. Do the same thing with the pepper. Don't use too much!

4 When the paint is *completely* dry (it may take three or four days), use your fingernail to peel it off the waxed paper.

PULL THE PRANK

1 Put the dropping on a car windshield or anywhere else a bird might do its business. You might need to put a small piece of rolled-up tape on the bottom to make it stay put.

2 If you decided to make a very large bird dropping—or you leave lots of smaller ones—get really excited when your victim discovers the poopy gift, and say that you recently heard a news report about a new variety of pigeon in the area that produces record-setting amounts of turds.

the prank

BEWARE!
This prank may cause a mess. Be prepared to clean up!

Fake dog poop is a prank that never seems to grow old (unlike real dog poop). In fact, the S. S. Adams Company (see page 75) first started selling rubber dog doo more than 70 years ago and hasn't stopped. You can make your own fake poop using the following recipe. Then leave a pile on the front stoop, the bathroom floor, or anyplace else where it will catch someone's attention. You can also use your fake dog doo to make a delicious "new" candy called Minturds (see page 54), using the cutout label on page 213.

what you need

* A bowl
* A tablespoon
* A mixing spoon
* 3 to 4 tablespoons peanut butter
* 4 tablespoons chocolate syrup
* 1 tablespoon flour
* Sugar (white or brown)

EW! WARNING

This prank is pretty gross, so choose your victim wisely. Pick someone who laughs hysterically at fart jokes and other bathroom humor—not the crank who gives you a withering look of disgust.

what you do

THE SETUP

1 In a bowl, mix the peanut butter and the chocolate syrup together. Add more syrup if you need to until it's the right shade of brown.

2 Gradually mix in the flour, adding small amounts until the mixture has the consistency of cookie dough.

3 Add a little sugar to give it texture.

4 Roll the mixture into pooplike logs.

PULL THE PRANK

1 Arrange the pieces of fake poop in a pile in the driveway, on top of your parents' car, or wherever else you think it will get noticed. Use your imagination. But also use your common sense: It's sticky stuff, so don't put it where it will be hard to clean up, like on a rug or sofa—or your sister's bed.

Ew! Dog Poop

MINTURDS

LABEL

DIFFICULTY LEVEL:

MEDIUM

IF I MAKE THE POOP LOGS SMALLER THEY LOOK LIKE LITTLE CANDIES.

ARE YOU SURE YOU DON'T WANT ANY? THAT MEANS MORE FOR ME! MMM-MMM!

the prank

Do you have a gullible friend or sibling who can't resist the allure of something new and exotic? Use the Minturds label to convince a friend that there is a brand-new, difficult-to-obtain candy made out of dog poop!

what you need

* Fake dog poop (see the recipe on page 53)
* Mint tin (Altoids or similar brand)
* "Minturds" label on page 213
* Scissors
* Tape or glue

EW! WARNING

This prank is pretty gross, so choose your victim wisely. Pick someone who laughs hysterically at fart jokes and other bathroom humor—not the crank who gives you a withering look of disgust.

what you do

THE SETUP

1 Make some fake dog poop using the recipe on page 53. Mold the fake poop into the shape of little candies.

2 Remove the mints from the tin and save them to eat later.

3 Carefully cut out the prank label for Minturds on page 213. Tape or glue it to the top of the container. Arrange your edible poop candies inside, and you're ready.

PULL THE PRANK

1 Walk up to a friend and ask if she would like to try some new candies. Display the cover of the tin and then open it. Tell your victim, "Minturds are a delicious new candy made from imported turds."

2 When your friend acts completely grossed out, pop one of the candies in your mouth and say, "Yum. So good!"

FART MACHINE

Prank #22

DIFFICULTY LEVEL:
EXPERT

OK, I'VE GOT THE PAPER CLIP SO IT FORMS A C-SHAPE...

DAD WILL HELP ME MAKE A U-SHAPE, ABOUT ONE INCH FROM THE END.

...AND NOW I ADD THE RUBBER BANDS AND THE WASHER

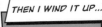

THEN I WIND IT UP...

WHOA, WHICH ONE OF YOU HAD THE BEAN BURRITO?

NOT ME!

BA-RAPPP!

the prank

When the Whoopee Cushion was invented in 1930 (see page 59), it added a whole new dimension to the ordinary act of sitting down. Since then, other flatulence-producing devices have been invented, including a remote-control version that Johnny Depp reportedly used on the set of *Pirates of the Caribbean: On Stranger Tides* every time Penélope Cruz went in for a close-up. You can add to your arsenal of pranks by making your own hand-operated fart machine.

what you need

ADULT HELP

* 1 large paper clip
* Pliers (optional)
* 2 medium-size rubber bands or hair elastics
* 1 keychain ring or 1-inch metal washer (available at hardware stores)
* A paperback book

what you do:

THE SETUP

1 Carefully unbend the paper clip until it forms a C shape.

2 **Ask an adult** to help you bend each end so it makes a 90-degree angle about 1 inch from the end. You can use your hands, but it's easier if you use pliers.

3 Now bend the ends back the other way to form little u-shaped hooks.

4 Pass each rubber band through the keychain ring or washer.

5 Hook the rubber bands over the bent ends of the paper clip.

6 Now wind up the washer until the rubber bands are twisted tight.

7 Practice using the fart machine until you get the best possible sound. Sit on a sofa or another cushioned seat and place the machine on a paperback book with your hand over it. You'll need to keep your hand pressed down to hold the wound-up washer in place. Lift your hand slightly so the washer starts flipping. Adjust how high you lift your hand to get the most authentic-sounding fart. You can also experiment with different sized washers to get lower- or higher-pitched sounds.

continues ➥

FART MACHINE
(continued)

PULL THE PRANK

1 Use your fart machine when you're hanging out with friends or family. Wind up the machine and hide it in your hand before you enter the room. Bring a paperback book with you, and casually set it down beside you. Place the hand with the fart machine facedown on the book.

2 Wait for a pause in the conversation and lift your hand slightly when you're ready to let it rip. Look at someone in the room or just away from your hand so you don't seem connected to the sound.

3 When people look in your direction or start laughing, there are several ways you can react. Here are a few examples:

* Act embarrassed and exclaim, "Excuse me!" Then leave the room with the machine hidden in your hand. Wind it up, return to the room, and "fart" again. Use your judgment as to how many times to repeat this.

* Look at the person next to you and say, "Whoa! What did you eat for lunch, dude?!"

* Act completely oblivious, as if nothing happened. Then leave the room, rewind your machine, and repeat.

Whoopee!

For the Whoopee Cushion!

Sometimes the best ideas for pranks happen when you're not even trying. The trick is to keep your mind open to the possibilities around you. That's what the workers at a rubber company did in 1930, and the results were explosive. Employees at the JEM Rubber Company in Toronto, Canada, were playing around with leftover pieces of rubber one day when they accidentally produced a sound much like a fart. The workers had so much fun playing with the homemade prank that the company decided to bring the idea to S. S. Adams, the pioneering manufacturer of gags and practical jokes (see page 75). Adams turned his nose up at the idea because he thought it was "indelicate," but he probably kicked himself later. Another company, Johnson Smith, took a chance on the rubber device. They called it a Whoopee Cushion and said it gave forth "noises that can be better imagined than described." It was music to the ears of delighted pranksters across the country. Sales took off—and they're still powerful to this day.

Scientist Trevor Cox tries out his giant whoopee cushion.

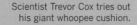

FINGER FREAK-OUT

DIFFICULTY LEVEL: EXPERT

STEP 1

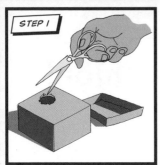

STEP 2

STEP 3

WANNA SEE SOMETHING AMAZING? MY UNCLE JOE WAS BORN WITH AN EXTRA FINGER AND HAD IT CUT OFF. WE'VE KEPT IT IN THE FAMILY FOR YEARS.

WHOA, DUDE!...

WOW! LEMME SEE.

GOTCH

the prank

Making this trick box takes some work, but once you get it right, you can use it again and again to fool people into thinking you found a "dead" finger. This prank is pretty gross, so choose your victim carefully. Do it on a friend or a grown-up with a good sense of humor and a strong stomach. In other words, don't try it on your baby sister who's afraid of kittens.

what you need

* A small cardboard jewelry box with a piece of cotton in the bottom and a lid (ask your mother or sister if she has one she doesn't need)
* Scissors
* Ketchup

ADULT HELP

what you do

THE SETUP

1 **Ask an adult** to help you cut a hole in the bottom of the box, almost in the center, but a little closer to one end. The hole should be just big enough for your middle finger or index finger to fit through.

2 Have the same adult help you cut a similar hole in the piece of cotton. When you put the cotton back in the box, the two holes should line up so you can stick your finger straight through both of them.

3 Hold the box in the palm of one hand and poke your middle finger or index finger through the hole. Then bend the finger so it lies down on the little bed of cotton. Use the other fingers of that hand to hold the edges of the box.

4 With your "dead" finger resting on the piece of cotton, use your other hand to put a little bit of ketchup on the

cotton near your finger. You can put some on the finger, too, but don't overdo it. A little looks real, a lot looks fake.

5 Now put the lid on the box, and you're ready to go.

PULL THE PRANK

1 With the trick box in your hand, walk up to your victim. Before showing the finger, tell a good story about how you got it. For instance, you could explain that your uncle was born with an extra finger and recently had to have it amputated. The doctor gave him the finger after surgery, and you borrowed it for the day.

2 Then ask if your friend would like to see it. Remove the lid and hold the box out for your friend to see. If you want to freak him out even more, let him stare at it for a while. Then move the "dead" finger ever so slightly.

Prank #24

DIFFICULTY LEVEL: EASY

OK, BEFORE BOBBY COMES DOWN FOR BREAKFAST, I'LL JUST SLIP THIS PRANK CARD INTO HIS FAVORITE CEREAL BOX...

WHAT'S THAT? IT SAYS YOU CAN WIN 1,000 DOLLARS!! WOW, READ IT OUT LOUD...

COOL!

MAYBE YOU SHOULD CHECK AGAIN... YOU MIGHT HAVE MISSED IT!!!

WHEW!

the prank

Breakfast cereal, like petroleum jelly, is just one of those things that inspires pranks. There are the classic tricks, like switching the contents of two different boxes of cereal, or replacing the cereal in one box with rice or pasta or plastic bugs. This cereal prank is a bit flakier—actually, a lot flakier—since you'll convince your victim to check every flake in the box for the "winning" piece. It's guaranteed to make your victim switch to eating toast in the morning.

what you need

* Scissors
* A box of your victim's favorite cereal
* Several bowls or one large bowl
* "Win $1,000" insert on page 213

what you do

THE SETUP

1 Carefully cut out the "Win $1,000" insert on page 213.

2 In the morning, before breakfast, sneak the insert into a box of your victim's preferred cereal.

PULL THE PRANK

1 When your victim pours a bowl of cereal and the paper falls out, play dumb but act curious. Ask him to read the paper out loud. It will instruct him to look for a flake with the winning number "7" printed on it to win $1,000. Then say, "Wow, cool! Let's see if you won!" That should get your victim to start sifting through the cereal, looking for the numbered piece. Bring out extra bowls so your victim can fill each one and search the whole box of cereal.

2 When your victim gets to the end of the box, act sympathetic: "Too bad, I guess you didn't get a box with the winning piece. You should get Mom or Dad to buy more." If you want to be really sneaky, say, "Maybe you should check again. You might have missed it."

DIFFICULTY LEVEL:
EXPERT

WOW! LOOK AT THIS COOL BUG I FOUND ON THIS FLOWER!

AHH!!! I THINK THE BUG JUST PEED ON ME!

SQUIRT

the prank

Nature is full of marvelous surprises—shooting stars, glow-in-the-dark fish, and squirting flowers. Squirting flowers? That's where you come in. You'll need to practice this prank a few times before you try it on someone. But once you master it, you can use it to create a splash with your nature-loving friends. You can substitute a leaf or a real-looking plastic bug for the flower.

what you need

* A small balloon (about 2 inches across)
* Scissors
* Water
* A small flower

what you do

THE SETUP

1 Cut off the long end of the balloon (the part you blow into) so just the round part is left.

2 At the sink, fill the balloon almost to the top with water.

3 This is the part that takes some practice: Hold your left hand with the palm facing up. Use your right hand to position the balloon under your left hand so the opening pokes up between two fingers. Press the two fingers together to grip the opening of the balloon. The rest of the balloon should hang down below your hand.

4 Place the flower on the open palm of your left hand. Then hold the water-filled part of the balloon gently with your right hand. (No one should be able to see the balloon; they should see just your open palm and the flower.)

PULL THE PRANK

1 Hold out your left hand with the flower and say to your victim, "Hey, I found this flower that has a really cool little insect on it. Don't touch it, but look at it. You have to get really close. It's amazing!" Encourage your victim to move in for a good view.

2 When the person's face is close to the flower, use your right hand to squeeze the hidden balloon. You may need to separate your fingers a little to let the water through. Your victim will get a surprise shower—from a flower!

Prank #26

DIFFICULTY LEVEL: EXPERT

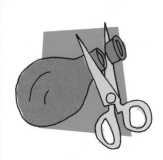

the prank

If you have a friend who appreciates a good gross-out, try this variation of the Flower Shower prank. A squirting blister definitely beats a squirting flower on the disgustingness scale.

what you need

* A small balloon (about 2 inches across)
* Scissors
* Water
* A small bandage

what you do

THE SETUP

1 Follow steps 1–3 of the Flower Shower prank on page 65.

2 Place a small bandage on your palm. Then hold the water-filled part of the balloon gently with your right hand. (No one should be able to see the balloon, just your open palm and the bandage.)

PULL THE PRANK

1 Hold out your left hand with the bandage and say to your victim, "I have this really weird blister on my hand. Take a look, it's right next to the bandage. It's kind of hard to see."

2 When they're in good and close, squeeze the balloon and say something like, "Oh, man, I think it just popped. I hope it didn't get in your eye!"

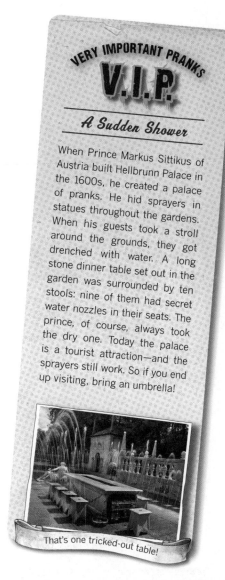

VERY IMPORTANT PRANKS

V.I.P.

A Sudden Shower

When Prince Markus Sittikus of Austria built Hellbrunn Palace in the 1600s, he created a palace of pranks. He hid sprayers in statues throughout the gardens. When his guests took a stroll around the grounds, they got drenched with water. A long stone dinner table set out in the garden was surrounded by ten stools: nine of them had secret water nozzles in their seats. The prince, of course, always took the dry one. Today the palace is a tourist attraction—and the sprayers still work. So if you end up visiting, bring an umbrella!

That's one tricked-out table!

the prank

Evergreens, maples, rhododendrons—all are beautiful trees and shrubs, but unfortunately none of them grows edible fruit. Until now, that is! Make your parents think they never quite grasped where fruit comes from with this juicy prank.

what you need

* 5 to 10 pieces of one kind of fruit (bananas, oranges, apples, strawberries, etc.)
* A large bush or a small tree that doesn't normally grow edible fruit
* String and/or tape

what you do

THE SETUP

1 Choose your tree or shrub and the type of fruit you want it to "grow." Make sure to take weight into account— meaning, don't tie oranges to a bush with flimsy branches.

2 When no one is watching, attach the fruit to the bush or tree using the string or tape. For heavier fruits without stems, like oranges, tie pieces of string around the middle of the fruit (the "equator") and knot them tightly. Add a piece of tape if necessary.

PULL THE PRANK

1 Wait for someone to notice the miracle of nature. You may need to direct their attention to the plant by saying something like, "Wow, that tree is finally producing some fruit!"

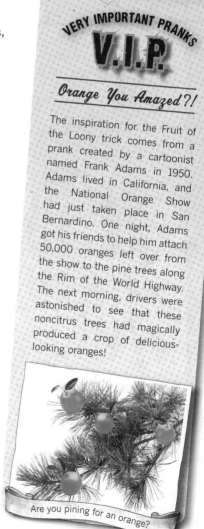

VERY IMPORTANT PRANKS

V.I.P.

Orange You Amazed?!

The inspiration for the Fruit of the Loony trick comes from a prank created by a cartoonist named Frank Adams in 1950. Adams lived in California, and the National Orange Show had just taken place in San Bernardino. One night, Adams got his friends to help him attach 50,000 oranges left over from the show to the pine trees along the Rim of the World Highway. The next morning, drivers were astonished to see that these noncitrus trees had magically produced a crop of delicious-looking oranges!

Are you pining for an orange?

the prank

The U.S. Women's National Soccer Team is known for its fancy footwork on the field. But in 2010, defender Heather Mitts pulled a fast one *off* the field with a prank known as the Funnel Game. Mitts and her co-conspirator, forward Natasha Kai, walked up to another teammate and asked if she wanted to play a new game. After showing their victim how it is played— you try to get a quarter resting on your closed eyelid into a funnel strategically placed inside the waistband of your pants—Mitts and Kai challenged her to try it. As soon as she closed her eyes, they poured water in the funnel—and down her pants. Try it on *your* "teammates." They might not think it's a winner, but you will!

what you need

* A plastic funnel
* A quarter
* A bottle of water

what you do

THE SETUP

1 Practice on a co-conspirator first to get the timing right. Then find a friend or sibling who's always up for a random game. It's best to pull the prank outdoors so you won't have to clean up the mess.

PULL THE PRANK

1 Approach your friend with the funnel and quarter. Make sure you have a bottle of water with you, but don't draw attention to it. Tell your friend that you learned a new game and get her to agree to play.

2 Explain the rules:
* Tell her to put the plastic funnel, narrow-end first, in the waistband of her pants.
* Next, tell her to close her eyes, tip her head back to face the sky, and put the quarter on her right eyelid.
* Then, tell her to tilt her head down, trying to get the quarter to fall in the funnel.

3 As soon as your victim closes her eyes and tips her head back, pour the bottle of water into the funnel.

4 RUN!

the prank

When little kids get a present they don't like, it's easy to tell: They start opening another present right away—or begin wailing because they wanted a new video game, not a book about the history of the vacuum cleaner. Grown-ups are different. They're trained to be polite. They say things like, "Well, this certainly looks *interesting*!" or "How did you ever come up with this idea?!" That's why you should pull this prank on a grown-up—parents, aunts or uncles, or grandparents. Do this prank when it's your victim's birthday or during a holiday like Christmas or Hanukkah that involves gifts. And remember the most important part: Make sure you keep a straight face! The second most important part? Getting your victim a *real* gift, too.

what you need

* A really stupid gift (more about that to follow)
* Wrapping paper
* Scissors
* Tape
* A card

what you do

THE SETUP

1 Before a holiday or your victim's birthday, search your house for a gift that the person would *never* want. Here are some ideas to get you in the spirit:

* For your grandmother: an action figure or a used paintbrush
* For your grandfather: a frilly umbrella or a half-empty bottle of shampoo

VERY IMPORTANT PRANKS

V.I.P.

Loony Clooney

If you are a pro at pranking, like actor George Clooney, you can keep a gift gag ruse going for a long time. Clooney once noticed a crummy old painting in a pile of garbage. He took the artwork home, cleaned it off, and signed his name at the bottom so it looked like he was the artist. Then he gave it to a good friend as a present. His friend put the painting on his wall to be polite, and it ended up staying there for two years before Clooney finally confessed to the hoax.

continues ➡

GAG GIFT
(continued)

* For your mother or aunt: a bottle of after-shave or slightly used men's shoes
* For your father or uncle: a stuffed animal or a box of crayons
* For anyone: a potato, a roll of paper towels, an empty plastic water bottle, one elastic hair tie, a toothbrush, or a tube of toothpaste
* If you can't find something at home, and you don't mind spending a little money, go to a store that sells cheap stuff and buy something completely ridiculous.

2 Wrap up the gift and add a ribbon if you have one.

3 Write your name on the card so your victim knows it's from you.

PULL THE PRANK

1 Present your gift to your victim at the appropriate occasion. When the person opens the gift, you *must* keep a straight face. Try to look sincere and pleased, like you picked out something very special. You can even say in a hopeful voice, "Do you like it?" if you can manage it without cracking up.

2 Before the disappointment *really* sinks in, give your victim their actual gift.

Gags for Sale

In 1904 a young man named Søren Sørensen was working as a dye salesman in New Jersey. His company had a problem: An ingredient in their dye gave people sneezing fits. But Sørensen didn't see a problem—he saw an opportunity. He tested some of the powder on a group of his friends, and soon they were all sneezing—and laughing. They asked for their own supplies to use on their friends. Sørensen quickly started bottling the powder and selling it as a prank under the name Cachoo Sneeze Powder. People loved it. In the first year, he sold 150,000 bottles—which gave him the money he needed to make other gags. He changed his name to Soren Sorensen Adams, and his new company, S. S. Adams, started supplying itching powder, snake-in-a-can pranks, and the bestselling Dribble Glass (that caused victims to spill their drink all over their shirt) to pranksters across the country. In 1928 he invented the Joy Buzzer, a tiny wind-up buzzer you hold in the palm of your hand and use to shock someone when you shake hands. It was a huge seller back then—and still is today.

During his long career, Adams invented more than 600 gags. He said his approach was to work with "an ordinary, everyday object, which is around the house." The company Adams founded still sells many of his ingenious inventions, and some of them inspired pranks in this book. You can make your own version of the Dribble Glass with a soda can (page 48), fake dog poop (page 52), a prank ice cube (page 90), and fake vomit (page 164).

Cartoonist Louis M. Glackens created illustrations for many of the S. S. Adams Company's novelties, giving the buyer an idea of how the gag played out.

the prank

Imagine looking out your window one snowy morning and seeing a GIANT footprint in the white-carpeted yard. You might be so freaked out that you crawl back under the covers and stay there! If you live where it snows, this prank is the perfect way to shock your family and your neighbors after a storm. If you don't live where it snows, try this prank at the beach using wet sand. All it takes is a little planning, imagination, and a shovel to get one rather large footprint.

what you need

* A pencil and paper
* A shovel

what you do

THE SETUP

1 Make a drawing of what you want the footprint to look like. Or wet the sole of a boot or sneaker and press it down on a piece of paper to create a print you can use as a guide.

2 Wait for a snowy day (or a day at the beach) and a time of day when there won't be many people around to see what you're up to.

PULL THE PRANK

1 Use the shovel to create the shape of one or more oversize footprints in the snow (or sand). Look at your drawing and visualize a bigger version of the footprint.

2 When you're finished making the oversize prints, get rid of your own tiny footprints. Start at the top of the giant footprint (farthest from the door to your house) and lightly rake your shovel over your footprints.

3 Act completely astonished when someone notices the giant print. If you pulled this prank in the snow, tell your little sibling that a Yeti must have passed through. If you pulled this prank at the beach, tell your little sibling that the Loch Ness monster must have walked out of the water wearing boots.

VERY IMPORTANT PRANKS
V.I.P.

The Original Giant Step

When a foot of snow fell in Edinburgh, Scotland, in 2010, Nial Smith didn't build a snowman in his backyard like everyone else did. He created what looked like the footprint of a boot-wearing giant. He made a sketch of the shape he wanted, and one hour later, the footprint filled his yard. When his neighbors looked out their windows, they probably thought it was time to leave town.

Nial Smith's fancy footwork.

the prank

Try this prank on October 31 and put the *trick* back into trick or treat. Choose a victim who no longer believes in monsters under the bed. In other words, don't try this prank on a little sibling who still does a running leap into bed every night to avoid whatever lurks below.

what you need

* A pair of jeans
* Towels, T-shirts, or other clothing that can get wrinkled, for stuffing
* Old newspapers or packing material
* Socks
* Shoes
* Safety pins

what you do

THE SETUP

1 Stuff the jeans with the towels or clothing. Move the stuffing around until it looks like there's a body inside the jeans.

2 Stuff the socks with newspaper or packing material so they look like someone's feet and ankles.

3 Put the shoes on the "feet," and tie the laces if necessary.

4 Your fake body is almost done. Just attach the "feet" to the pants legs using the safety pins. Arrange it so the pins don't show.

Hang on just a minute!

PULL THE PRANK

1 Place the "severed body" under the bed so the legs stick out enough to scare the pants off your victim.

2 When you hear the person scream, run in and scream yourself, as if you're seeing the body for the first time. Then you should probably show your victim some mercy by shouting "Happy Halloween!"

the prank

Halloween is the perfect time to pull pranks that have a creepy edge. If someone in your family takes especially long and steamy showers, this prank is perfect for him or her—especially if you pull it on the scariest day of the year. With nothing more than lemon juice and a cotton swab, you can make a ghostly message appear in the bathroom mirror while your victim is showering away.

what you need

* A cotton swab or cotton ball
* Lemon juice

what you do

THE SETUP

1 First decide what message you want to appear on the mirror. Shorter is better: HELP! or WATCH OUT! or I SEE YOU or I WANT YOUR BLOOD! are all good. Or just write the name of someone in the family.

2 Now dip the cotton swab (or a small piece of the cotton ball) in the lemon juice. Squeeze out the excess juice so it won't drip when you write. Then use the cotton to write your message on the mirror in big letters.

PULL THE PRANK

1 Wait for your victim to take a shower and steam up the bathroom. When the person looks in the mirror, your ghostly message will be waiting there.

VERY IMPORTANT PRANKS

V.I.P.

Zombie Alert!

Commuters in Austin, Texas, probably thought they were still in bed dreaming when they read the electronic signs at a busy intersection one Monday morning in 2009. ZOMBIES AHEAD! said one sign. RUN FOR YOUR LIVES! warned another. Pranksters had hacked the computers in the signs and changed the message from CONSTRUCTION AHEAD to the zombie alert. The new messages didn't last for long, though: A construction manager saw the signs on his way to work and quickly had them changed back.

Sign of zombies in Austin, Texas.

the prank

Your parents probably like it when you do your homework instead of playing video games (or pulling pranks). They might even like it when you ask them for help. But after they've tried to solve these infuriatingly impossible math problems, they may want to take a nice, long break from homework assignments.

what you need
* Math homework handout on page 205

what you do

THE SETUP

1 Carefully cut out the math homework handout on page 205. (You can photocopy or scan it at a larger size if you want it to look even more authentic or print one out at workman.com/pranklopedia.)

2 Fill in your name and the date.

PULL THE PRANK

1 Give the fake homework sheet to a parent and explain that you are having trouble and would like some help. Keep a straight face when·your parent starts struggling to figure out the answers. The problems all sound normal, but they're actually impossible to solve!

2 You can add to your parent's frustration by saying something like:
* "Our teacher said we should be able to do all of the problems in twenty minutes or less."
* "Maybe you're not reading the problem carefully enough. I think you're rushing."
* "Wow, now I know why I'm no good at math. It must be genetic."

the prank

There are lots of websites that offer homework help, but only one that helps with homework *pranks*. Fake out your friends or siblings by sending them a link to this completely different homework site.

what you need

* Access to a computer for you and a friend or a sibling

what you do

THE SETUP

1 Wait for a day when you think your homework is particularly challenging or when you know your sibling has a difficult assignment.

2 If you want to see your victims' reactions, send them the link when you are all in the same room with access to computers.

PULL THE PRANK

1 Send your friends or sibling an email saying, "I found this great website—workman.com/homeworkhelp—that helps you with homework." When they go to the website they'll be in for a big surprise.

the prank

Ice cream is like summer vacation: Just thinking about it can make you feel good—unless it's *this* ice cream. It looks like the real thing—perfect scoops of chocolate and strawberry ice cream. But it tastes like something you might use to clean drains.

what you need

- Instant mashed potatoes (plain or garlic)
- Water
- A microwave
- Chocolate syrup
- Cocoa powder (optional)
- Cinnamon
- Nutmeg
- Worcestershire sauce (optional)
- Red food coloring
- Yellow mustard
- A microwave-proof bowl
- A teaspoon
- A serving spoon
- 2 bowls for serving
- Real chocolate or strawberry ice cream for you!

what you do

THE SETUP

1 Mix the instant mashed potatoes with water. (Follow the directions on the package.) **Ask an adult** to help you microwave the mixture for three minutes.

2 Let the mixture cool. While you're waiting, decide if you want to make "chocolate" or "strawberry." If you prefer to make both flavors, put half of the potato mix in a second bowl so you can create the flavors separately.

To make "chocolate ice cream":

Mix the following ingredients into the potato mixture:

- A couple tablespoons of chocolate syrup
- 1 tablespoon cocoa powder (optional)
- 1 tablespoon of cinnamon
- 1 tablespoon of nutmeg

Stir and taste a tiny bit to make sure it's awful. You can also add Worcestershire sauce if you have some.

To make "strawberry ice cream":

Stir 1 drop of red food coloring and 1 tablespoon of mustard into the potato mixture. If the color isn't red enough, mix in one drop of food coloring at a time until it's the right shade.

ICE CREAM THAT MAKES YOU SCREAM

(continued)

PULL THE PRANK

1 When your victim isn't around, use an ice-cream scoop or a spoon to shape the fake ice cream into scoops and arrange them in a serving bowl. Put some real ice cream in a similar bowl for yourself.

2 For added authenticity you can save an empty container from real chocolate or strawberry ice cream. Put your fake ice cream in the container and stick it in the freezer just before you're ready to serve it. Make sure your victim sees you take it out and scoop it into a bowl. And be sure to take *your* serving from a container of the real stuff.

3 Serve your victim the ice cream and act completely shocked when she spits it out in disgust.

Improv Everywhere:

Everybody, Freeze!

Most pranksters work alone or with one or two co-conspirators. Improv Everywhere thinks bigger—*much* bigger. The group organizes hundreds of people to stage pranks in public places, usually to the delight of bystanders. Comedian and prankster Charlie Todd founded the group in 2001. In one of its best-known pranks, 207 people gathered at Grand Central Terminal, the world's largest train station, in New York City. At a prearranged time, they all froze in place for five minutes. One prankster was in the middle of eating a hot dog. Two people were in the middle of a kiss. Commuters and tourists passing through the station were completely baffled. It looked like someone had pressed the PAUSE button on a video camera. Luckily, volunteers were busy pressing the RECORD button and they captured reactions. The prank has received more than 29 million views on YouTube, and it has been re-created in more than 100 cities around the world.

In another Improv Everywhere prank, the "Human Mirror," sets of twins sat down across from each other in a New York City subway car, making it look like one side of the car was a mirror image of the other. The group also once turned a Little League baseball game in Hermosa Beach, California, into a major-league event. They filled the normally empty stands with rabid, paint-covered fans, printed glossy programs with photos of all the players, and got NBC Sports to install a Jumbotron screen in the outfield and send in a famous sportscaster to call the game. The prank was an out-of-the-park home run.

Twin pranksters turned a New York City subway car into a human mirror.

Prank #36

DIFFICULTY LEVEL: **EASY**

OKAY, I'M DONE DROPPING THE FAKE TURDS INTO THE ICE.

HEY, WANT SOME WATER?

AWESOME, THANKS...

OH MY GOSH, WE HAD A MOUSE PROBLEM FOR A WHILE... BUT HOW COULD THE TURDS HAVE GOTTEN IN THE ICE CUBE TRAY?

GULP!

the prank

What's more disgusting than finding a fly in your drink? Finding a mouse turd in your drink. This prank is a variation on a classic store-bought gag—a plastic ice cube with an insect inside. It works best if you put the ice cubes in water or a light-colored drink, so the "turds" really stand out.

what you need

* An ice cube tray
* A toothpick (optional)
* About 20 dried currants (Currants look like baby raisins. Look for them near the raisins at the supermarket. If you can't find them, buy raisins and ask an adult to help you cut them into smaller pieces.)

what you do

THE SETUP

1 Fill an ice cube tray with water. Place it in the freezer and leave it until the ice cubes are half-frozen.

2 Remove the ice cubes from the freezer and use a toothpick or your finger to poke a hole in the top of each one.

3 Drop one or two currants or raisin bits into the hole. They should sink about halfway down.

4 Return the ice cubes to the freezer. When they're completely frozen, it's time to pull the prank.

PULL THE PRANK

1 Prepare cold drinks for yourself and your victim. Put regular ice cubes in your drink and put the "special" ice cubes in your victim's drink.

2 Act really concerned and a little embarrassed when your victim notices the brown stuff in the ice cubes. Say something like, "Oh my gosh, you know we had a mouse problem for a while, but how could the turds have gotten in the ice cube tray?" Or say, "Oh, whatever, I'll take those!" and spoon the icky ice cubes into your glass.

Alan Abel:

Indecent Animals?

During the 1960s and 1970s, prankster Alan Abel convinced people that hundreds of publicity stunts he made up were true events. One was a campaign to get animals to wear clothes. Abel wrote to several magazines and explained that he wanted to relieve animals of the shame they felt from living life in the nude. To his amazement, magazine editors took him seriously. So Abel kept going with the hoax. He hired an actor to appear on TV talk shows as the president of the campaign. Abel received 40,000 letters of support before *Time* magazine finally exposed the prank in 1963. Besides entertaining the public, Abel had a message: Don't believe everything you see, hear, or read.

Intelligence Test:

Do Pranks Make People Smarter?

S **cientists are still** learning how the human brain works. In 2010, a Polish neuroscientist discovered that pulling pranks can actually make you smarter. Dr. Fran Luschinsky has been studying the effects of pranks on the brain since 1999. Her research shows that people who pull at least one prank a week grow twice as many new brain cells as nonpranksters. They also have higher IQ scores, earn more money, and report being happier.

Luschinsky says that while doing her research, she discovered another way to make your brain cells grow faster that you can do at home. She says you may actually *feel* your brain getting bigger as you do it. Try it yourself:

1. Take a grapefruit, a large orange, or an apple and balance it on top of your head. This may take some practice.

2. Walk slowly back and forth across the room while saying the word *knarp* (pronounced KUH-NARP) each time you take a step.

How does this method work? Luschinsky offers a partial explanation: "The vitamins in the fruit are able to enter your brain cells because you are concentrating so hard," she says, before collapsing in a fit of giggles.

the prank

In 1870 a man named Robert Chesebrough started selling a gooey substance called petroleum jelly as a cure for dry skin, diaper rash, and other skin problems. The stuff is so perfect for doing pranks, it's hard to believe that's not what Chesebrough really had in mind when he invented it. Petroleum jelly is slippery but it stays put, it's practically colorless, and it feels gross when you touch it. Put it on something that a person touches every day without thinking—like a doorknob. Just be careful not to get it on fabric or anything else that can get stained.

what you need

* A jar of petroleum jelly (Vaseline or another brand)

what you do

THE SETUP

1. Choose an object in the house to grossify. A doorknob, the refrigerator door handle, a hairbrush handle, or a toothbrush handle are all good candidates. The toilet seat is a classic target, especially for sleepovers.

2. Spread a thin coating of the petroleum jelly on the object.

PULL THE PRANK

1. Wait for your victim to touch the slimy stuff and scream (or come looking for you). A word of caution: If you slime the toilet seat, make sure you don't forget an hour later and sit down on it yourself. You will become the "butt" of your own joke.

the prank

Without going to the trouble of starting a canned goods company, you can create new, "delicious" products to plant in your family's kitchen cabinets. How about some Cream of Sparrow Soup for lunch, or a nice bowl of Cream of Pink Soup for dinner? Maybe your favorite pooch would enjoy a special treat of Sneaky Snacks Dog Food. These are truly one-of-a-kind taste sensations.

what you need

* Soup or dog food label on pages 219–221
* Scissors
* Soup or dog food can
* Tape

what you do

THE SETUP

1 Choose which label you want to use from pages 219–221 and carefully cut it out.

2 Find a soup can in your kitchen cabinet that's the right size for the label you want to use. (A 6-ounce tomato paste can or other 6-ounce can works best for the labels in this book. For larger cans use the labels at workman.com/pranklopedia.) Tape the label to the can.

PULL THE PRANK

1 Put the can back in the cupboard and wait for someone to discover the new variety of soup or dog food in a single-serve can.

2 If you want to hurry things along, tell your parent you really want to have soup for supper or that the dog seems very hungry.

KNOT YOUR DAY

Prank #39

DIFFICULTY LEVEL: EASY

the prank

This prank is perfect for anyone you know who is always rushing around—especially in the morning, racing to get to work or school on time. Force your victim to slow down and smell the roses—or at least smell his sneakers, as he struggles to put them on.

what you need

* Your victim's lace-up shoes or sneakers

what you do

THE SETUP

1 When your victim isn't around, sneak into his room and find a pair of his favorite lace-up shoes or sneakers. Pull the laces until the shoes are closed tight.

2 Tie a small knot in each lace near the eyelet where your victim won't see it.

PULL THE PRANK

1 Watch as your victim tries to loosen the laces to put on the shoes—it will *knot* be easy!

LOONY LABELS

Prank #40

DIFFICULTY LEVEL: EASY

the prank

Food companies are always "improving" their products and adding labels to tell you how much tastier, healthier, or cheaper the newest version is. These new and improved product labels will make everything in your kitchen "NEW!" "IMPROVED!" and "RIDICULOUS!"

what you need

* "Loony Labels" on page 211
* Scissors
* Tape or glue

what you do

THE SETUP

1 Carefully cut out the "Loony Labels" on page 211.

2 Tape or glue the labels on milk cartons, cereal or cookie boxes, or other packaged foods in your family's kitchen.

PULL THE PRANK

1 If people fail to notice the new, improved labels, get their attention by holding up the product and saying something like, "I wonder if this tastes different now that they got rid of the spider eggs."

DIFFICULTY LEVEL:
MEDIUM

the prank

Some people demand a lot of attention the second they enter a room. This prank is perfect for pulling on friends or relatives who think they should be greeted with fanfare. All you need are some pots and pans and string to make your victim's entrance a smashing event.

what you need

* String
* Scissors
* 3 or more pots and pans that have a hole or loop in the handle (or use other nonbreakable objects you can tie a string to)

what you do

THE SETUP

1 Choose a room that your victim walks into a lot. Make sure the room has a door that your victim will *pull*, not push, to open.

2 Take the string, scissors, and pots and pans into the room and close the door. Place the pots and pans on tables, chairs, or shelves in the room, not too far from the door.

3 Cut a piece of string for each pot. The string should be long enough to reach from the pot to the doorknob—plus about 12 inches extra.

4 Tie one end of each piece of string to the doorknob. Tie the other ends to the pots. Make sure the string is slightly loose so it doesn't yank the pot off its perch.

PULL THE PRANK

1 Wait for your victim to walk into the room and unleash a cacophony of crashes. If you can't stand waiting and your victim is within earshot, call out that you need help with something and to come right away.

VERY IMPORTANT PRANKS
V.I.P.

Car Trouble

James Thurber is considered by many to be the funniest writer America has ever produced. He was also a practical joker, possibly thanks to his mother and his brother, Roy, both of whom loved inventing pranks. One of Roy's best jokes took advantage of the fact that his father was very nervous about the family's car. Whenever they went for a drive, he worried that the engine would suddenly explode. One day Roy gathered up every metal pot, pan, knife, fork, and other kitchen utensil he could find. He wrapped them in a piece of canvas, which he attached to the bottom of the car with a piece of string. He got into the driver's seat, holding one end of the string, and the family took off on their drive. As soon as he saw his father relax and close his eyes, Roy twitched the string. The metal clattered to the street with a deafening noise. "Stop the car!" the father yelled. "I can't," Roy answered. "The engine fell out." "Almighty!" the father gasped.

the prank

It's your lucky day. You just won $3,000 and an all-expenses-paid trip to beautiful, historic Transylvania! Use the "winning" ticket on page 213 to fool your friends into thinking you have exceptional good luck.

what you need

* "Winning Lottery Ticket" on page 213
* Scissors

what you do

THE SETUP

1 Carefully cut out the "Lucky Lottery Ticket" on page 213.

PULL THE PRANK

1 Run up to your victim waving the fake lottery ticket in one hand and act very excited. Make up a story about how a relative gave you the ticket as a present and when you scratched off all the numbers, you found out that you won $3,000 and a trip for two to Transylvania.

2 If you're feeling really generous, you can offer to invite your victim along so she, too, can enjoy a private dinner with Dracula, a stay at Transylvania's top school for vampires-in-training, fang implants, and all the blood smoothies she can drink.

the prank

Hearing your parents cry over spilled milk is no fun. But watching them cry over *fake* spilled milk is pretty entertaining (for you, at least). Just use puff paint from a craft store and glue to mix up one big, fake mess.

what you need

* White puff paint
* White glue (Elmer's glue or a similar brand)
* A disposable cup (paper or plastic)
* A stick or plastic spoon
* Waxed paper

what you do

THE SETUP

1 First make the "milk." Mix together about ¼ cup puff paint and ¼ cup glue with a stick or a plastic spoon in the disposable cup.

2 Carefully pour some of the paint onto a piece of waxed paper until you have a small puddle. Place the cup on its side at the edge of the puddle so it looks like the liquid just spilled out.

3 Let the paint dry *completely*. That could take three to four days.

Alternate method

You can skip the cup and just pour some paint on waxed paper and let it dry for a few days. Then peel it off and place it next to a half-full glass of milk.

PULL THE PRANK

1 When the paint is completely dry, carefully peel the spill *and* the cup off the waxed paper, using your fingernail to get it started.

2 Leave the fake spill (including the overturned cup) on the kitchen table or counter where someone will see it. Press down the edges of the spill if necessary.

3 Wait nearby so you can hear your victim's reaction. For extra entertainment, run in, grab a sponge or paper towel, and hand it to your victim. See if you can get the person to try to clean up the fake spill.

the prank

Penn Jillette and his partner, Teller, are master magicians. They also excel at inventing pranks to do in public places, such as restaurants, airports, and movie theaters. They must have been bored while waiting for a movie to begin when they thought up this trick. It takes a little work to set up, but the reaction you get is guaranteed to be more entertaining than whatever movie you're watching. (For another brilliant prank from this duo, see page 110.)

what you need

* A large tub or bag of popcorn
* A pen or pencil

what you do

THE SETUP

1 Buy a tub or bag of popcorn before the movie begins.

2 You need to tear a hole the size of your fist in the side of the tub or bag without your victim noticing. You can do it in the seat while waiting for the movie to start. Chat with your victim to keep him distracted from what you are doing. The hole should be just big enough for your fist to fit through, but no bigger.

* If you have a tub, hold it on your lap and use a pen or pencil to poke a hole through the side, close to the bottom. That will help you get the hole started. Then use your hand to finish tearing a hole.

* If you have a bag of popcorn, you won't need a pen to get the hole started.

3 Once you have made the fist-size hole, stick one arm through it so your hand sticks up into the tub but is hidden by the popcorn. Having your arm in the hole will keep the popcorn from spilling out.

PULL THE PRANK

1 While watching the movie, use your free hand to eat some popcorn yourself. Then offer some to your victim.

2 When your victim sticks his hand in the tub, grab it with your hand that's hidden in the popcorn. Hopefully you are at a scary movie and your victim's scream won't seem too out of place.

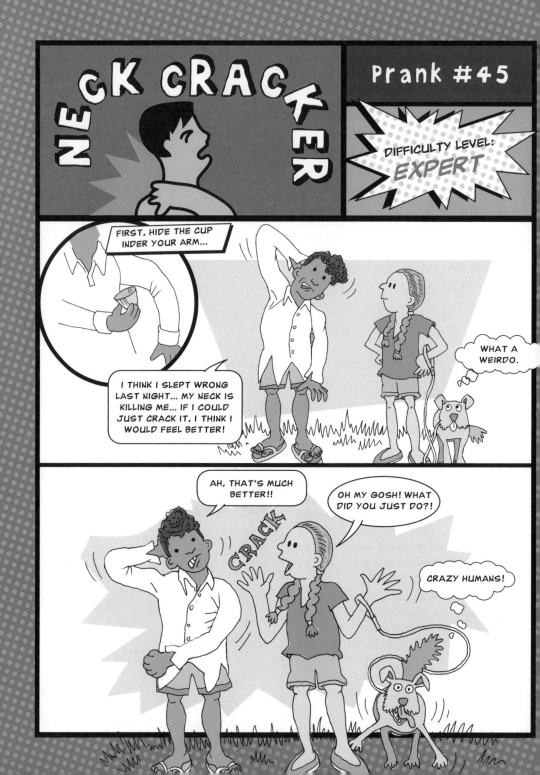

the prank

As you spend time developing your skills as a prankster, some grouch might tell you that pranks are a waste of time, that you should learn a practical skill like computer programming or knitting. "You can't make a living doing pranks," the curmudgeon might tell you. Actually, if you follow in the footsteps of two guys named Penn & Teller, you can. Besides performing magic shows for sold-out audiences, the devious duo has invented some of the best pranks ever. Most are pretty complicated to pull off. But this one just takes some practice. The trick is to use your armpit to crack a plastic cup while stretching your neck. When you get it right, your victim will think you just cracked your neck so hard you broke it. (For another Penn & Teller prank, see page 108.)

what you need
* A disposable cup made of hard plastic

what you do

THE SETUP

1 First, practice cracking the cup under your arm. Wear a loose, long-sleeved shirt so the cup won't show. Place the cup under your armpit, outside your shirt. Let your arm hang down by your side in a natural position. Now squeeze your arm against your side until you hear the cup crack. Stop when you hear the loud cracking sound.

2 Once you get good at cracking the cup with your arm in a natural position, you're ready to add the other half of the action: neck stretching. Slowly turn and tilt your head from side to side as if you're trying to loosen your neck muscles. After you have turned your head a few times, turn it one last time like you're giving your neck muscles one last really good stretch. As you do that, crack the hidden cup with your arm. You'll probably need to practice this a few times to get the timing right, so it sounds like you just cracked something in your neck.

PULL THE PRANK

1 Approach your victim with the cup hidden under your arm. Rub the back of your neck with your free hand and say something like, "My neck has been killing me all day. I think I slept on it the wrong way. I feel like if I could crack it just the right way, it would feel better. But I just can't seem to do it."

2 Now start turning and tilting your head, and on the last big stretch, crack the cup and say, "Ahhh . . . that feels much better." You'll be rewarded with a look of horror!

DIFFICULTY LEVEL: MEDIUM

DAD, THANKS FOR HELPING ME POUR THE HOT STUFF. NOW, WE'RE SUPPOSED TO STIR...

THERE IS NO WAY PRANKING MOM CAN BACKFIRE...

JUST NEED TO KEEP THIS IN THE FRIDGE OVERNIGHT...

MOM, I JUST POURED YOU SOME JUICE.

OH, THANKS HON...

the prank

This breakfast prank works best on someone who drinks orange juice every morning. Prepare the prank juice the night before, using your victim's usual glass. Then set it on the table in the morning. It will wake up your victim much faster than coffee.

what you need

* A box of lemon gelatin mix (Jell-O or similar brand)
* Water
* A bowl
* A spoon
* Orange juice

what you do

THE SETUP

1 **Ask an adult** to help you with the first step of the gelatin-making process—the part where you add one cup of boiling water to the mix and stir. Once you have done this step, stop!

2 Instead of adding cold water to the gelatin mixture, add one cup of cold orange juice and stir.

3 Pour some of the mixture into the glass your victim normally uses for OJ. Put the glass in the refrigerator and leave it there until it is completely solid. You need at least four hours, but overnight works best.

PULL THE PRANK

1 In the morning, put the glass of solid OJ on the table when your victim isn't looking. Watch her freak out when she tries to take the first sip of the juice and it won't budge from the bottom of the glass. If you're drinking OJ too, you can say, "Weird. Mine is fine!"

Ready to play outside?

Outdoor Art Pranks

Take a walking tour of outdoor paintings and sculptures with a sneaky sense of humor. These works of art aren't meant to be pranks, but they trick you and make you laugh the way a prank does!

SHARK ATTACK!

A house in Oxford, England, looks like it was attacked by a flying shark, thanks to sculptor John Buckley. He created a 25-foot shark out of lightweight fiberglass in 1986, at the request of Bill Heine, who owned the house. Buckley took his inspiration from the sharks he had seen on a trip to the Red Sea in Egypt. They reminded him of missiles used in wartime. He decided to have his shark plunge through the roof like a missile. Scary stuff! Back then, people either loved it or hated it. These days the shark mostly makes people smile. In 2009 it was even nominated as an "Icon of England."

John Buckley's fish out of water.

TURNING ART ON ITS HEAD

Visitors walking for the first time past the statue of Charles La Trobe on the campus of La Trobe University in Melbourne, Australia, probably do a double take: La Trobe is balancing on his head, and the "stone" pedestal that should be supporting him is pointing straight up at the sky. Did some campus pranksters flip Mr. La Trobe over during the night? No. The "prankster" is sculptor Charles Robb, and he designed the sculpture upside down on purpose, using lightweight plastic and fiberglass painted to look like bronze.

When the statue was first installed in 2007, some people thought it was disrespectful toward La Trobe, who was the first governor of the Australian state of Victoria. But the artist explains that he was thinking about the role universities play in helping people see things in new ways, "turning ideas on their heads." He certainly gave La Trobe a new view of the world.

WHEN SEEING IS NOT BELIEVING

German artist Edgar Müller and American artist John Pugh paint 3-D scenes on pavement. Called *trompe l'oeil* (that's French for "trick of the eye"), this style of painting tricks your eye into thinking the scene is real. Müller created this Ice Age crevasse on a pier in Dun Laoghaire, Ireland, in 2008. Watch your step!

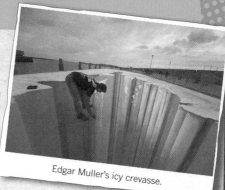
Edgar Muller's icy crevasse.

It looks like there is an ancient colonnade inside this "damaged" building in Los Gatos, California. In reality, it is all the work of John Pugh.

John Pugh's ancient trick.

French designer Benoit Lemoine created tape with a zipper pattern on it. He puts it on objects like trees and streetlamps and suddenly, they look like they need to be zipped up.

Benoit Lemoine's tree zipper.

Anderson Augusto and Leonardo Delafuente watch where they step.

Brazilian artists Anderson Augusto and Leonardo Delafuente transformed a manhole cover on a street in São Paulo, Brazil, into a giant watch.

Mark Jenkins makes sculptures of people out of packing tape. Then he dresses them and puts them in public places, doing unusual things like sticking their heads in walls.

Mark Jenkins's hidden head.

PARADE of FOOLS

DIFFICULTY LEVEL: **MEDIUM**

THE EMAIL PRANKSTER STRIKES AGAIN!!

Hey guys!

Looks like we're gonna have that April Fools' Day parade, again this

ONE WEEK LATER...

HEY NICE TIGHTY-WHITEYS!

HOPE MY MOM DOESN'T MISS HER BRA...

WHEN DOES THE PARADE START?

LIEMAN RD.

the prank

Every year, noted prankster Joey Skaggs alerts the media that an April Fools' Day parade will take place along Fifth Avenue in New York City. And every year, at least one reporter shows up looking for the big event. There's only one problem: The parade doesn't exist. Skaggs has duped CNN, *USA Today*, and many other media outlets into falling for the annual hoax. See if you can follow in his footsteps and convince your friends to show up for a parade in your town—it can be a parade in honor of April Fools' Day or some other occasion you dream up.

what you need

✳ An official-looking email that you can forward to your friends

what you do

THE SETUP

1 Type up an email to your friends that includes a fake forwarded email from the coordinator of this year's April Fools' Day parade. You can use the example on page 118 or write your own. Make sure to personalize your email with a note from you before the "forwarded" part.

2 See how far you can take the prank by telling your friends that if they want to march in the parade, they should arrive wearing their underwear outside their pants. Or make up your own insane instructions.

PULL THE PRANK

1 Once you've put the finishing touches on your email, send it to a bunch of your friends.

2 You may have to think fast if they respond with questions. For instance, if they say they looked online for more information about the parade and didn't find any, tell them it's an invitation-only event, or that the organizer is not Web-savvy.

3 If you succeed in convincing some of your friends that the the event is real, make sure you show up at start of the "parade route" to witness their embarrassment in person.

continues ➭

PARADE OF FOOLS
(continued)

sample email

Use this example or make up your own. If you use this one, fill in the date, time, town, and street names before you send it.

Hey guys,
Looks like there is going to be an April Fools' Day parade this year. I'm definitely going. You should too! Check it out.

On [date] at [time], Thomas Skeeter <tommy@skeeteropolis.not> wrote:

Dear Friends,

I am extremely pleased to announce that I am coordinating the first annual April Fools' Day parade in [insert your town]. It is the purest celebration of creativity and hilarity that I can imagine. If you would like to join us for the procession, please assemble at the corner of [insert street name] and [insert intersecting street name] at [time] sharp. I encourage you to wear your most foolish attire.

I hope you'll be able to join us!

Sincerely,

Thomas Skeeter
Coordinator, The April Fools' Day Parade

THE PRANKSTER HALL OF FAME

Joey Skaggs:

Father of the April Fools' Day Parade

Artist Joey Skaggs is probably the closest thing there is to a career prankster. He's been duping the public for more than 40 years. Skaggs specializes in media hoaxes: He stages fake events that sound real and convinces TV and newspaper reporters to cover them. Every April Fools' Day, he gets reporters to search for a nonexistent parade in New York City. In 1986, Skaggs announced he had invented a new weight-loss method called the Fat Squad. For $300 a day, you could hire a big, tough guy to follow you around day and night and use force, if necessary, to keep you from eating foods you shouldn't. The media "ate" up the story. Major newspapers wrote about the Fat Squad, and Skaggs even appeared on *Good Morning America* with fake goons before someone realized it was all a big fat hoax.

Joey Skaggs posing as Joe Bones, proprietor of the Fat Squad.

119

DIFFICULTY LEVEL: EASY

YEAH. MR WHISKERS DOESN'T LIKE TO COME OUT WHEN I HAVE COMPANY OVER.

WOW, AN AWARD FROM THE PRESIDENT FOR YOUR PET... I DIDN'T EVEN KNOW YOU HAD A PET?!

the prank

Like most people, you probably think your pet is the sweetest, smartest, most superb animal in the world. Now you can prove it by displaying an official Presidential Pet Achievement Award. Your pet will puff up with pride when it hears the news.

what you need

* "Presidential Pet Achievement Award" on page 223
* Scissors

what you do

THE SETUP

1 Carefully cut out the "Presidential Pet Achievement Award" on page 223.

2 Neatly print your pet's name and your family's last name in the two blank spaces provided.

PULL THE PRANK

1 Put the certificate in a place where friends and family will see it. Tell them only five pets receive the prestigious award each year!

PHONE FUN!

Prank #49

DIFFICULTY LEVEL: EASY

WRAP RUBBER BANDS AROUND THE TARGET'S PHONE.

ALMOST DONE!

HEY, RACHEED!! I THINK YOU HAVE A CALL!!

WHAAA

the prank

Do you have a relative or friend who is constantly checking her phone for texts, Tweets, or Facebook updates? Pull this prank on someone who is obsessed with his or her phone and hates to miss a single communication. You'll need lots of rubber bands, so save them up or buy a bunch at the store.

what you need

✳ About 20 to 30 rubber bands

what you do

THE SETUP

1 Find a time when you can get access to your victim's phone without the person seeing.

2 Wrap the rubber bands around the phone until it's completely covered.

PULL THE PRANK

1 Put the phone back where you found it and stick around to watch the show when the next call comes in. To speed things up, you can dial the victim's number yourself.

VERY IMPORTANT PRANKS
V.I.P.

A Phone Prank Fit for a Queen

When the Queen of England needed to set up the voicemail on her cell phone in 2007, she did the natural thing: She asked her tech-savvy grandsons, Harry and William, for help. The two princes also did the natural thing: They pranked their grandmother. Harry and William reportedly recorded an outgoing message on Queen Elizabeth's phone that said: "Wassup! This is Liz. Sorry I'm away from the throne. For a hotline to Philip, press one. For Charles, press two. And for the corgis, press three." (Philip is the queen's husband, Charles is her son, and the corgis are her beloved dogs.)

At first the Queen did not find the joke funny. But then she relaxed and saw the humor—especially when she pictured important people hearing the message. The Queen's secretary did not agree: He reportedly almost fell off his chair the first time his call was put through to the royal voicemail.

Presidential Pranks

A **sense of humor** isn't required to become president, but it doesn't hurt. Several U.S. presidents pulled impressive pranks when they were kids—and some saw no reason to stop once they made it to the White House.

Abraham Lincoln

ABRAHAM LINCOLN

When it came to humor, Abraham Lincoln (president from 1860–1865) was more famous for telling funny stories than pulling pranks. But when he was a young man still living at home, he was a trickster. One of his best pranks took advantage of his height: He was 6 feet, 4 inches tall and got teased a lot about it—especially by his stepmother. The story goes that she would tell him he'd better keep his head clean or she'd have to scrub the ceiling. One day when his stepmother was away, Lincoln saw two boys playing barefoot in the mud and got the idea for a prank. He brought the boys back to the house and held them upside down so their muddy feet could touch the ceiling. Then he had them "walk" across the ceiling, making a trail of brown footprints. The story goes that when his stepmother came home, she laughed so hard she couldn't get mad at him. But she did make Lincoln repaint the ceiling.

Calvin Coolidge

CALVIN COOLIDGE

Calvin Coolidge (president from 1923–1929) got his nickname, Silent Cal, by keeping his mouth shut, so it makes sense that his White House pranks were usually wordless. Coolidge had a series of buttons on his desk that he used to summon his staff. He liked to press all the buttons at once and watch people come running from all directions. He also liked to slip out the front door of the White House, press the alarm button near the door, and then go back inside to watch the Secret Service men come running up the walk to find out what was wrong. Coolidge enjoyed this trick so much, he would do it several times in a row. One can only guess how the Secret Service guys felt about it.

FRANKLIN D. ROOSEVELT

Franklin D. Roosevelt (president from 1933–1945), known as FDR, was famous for his sense of humor and he loved to play practical jokes. He got started young, pranking the governesses who took care of him. One of his early tricks involved his governess's chamber pot (a container people used to keep next to their beds in case they had to pee during the night). Young Franklin sneaked into his governess's bedroom and put a few spoonfuls of effervescent powder in her chamber pot. Later that night, she used the chamber pot and the powder started to hiss and bubble. The governess woke up everyone in the household, upset that there was something wrong with her.

Franklin Delano Roosevelt

HARRY S. TRUMAN

Harry S. Truman

Harry S. Truman (president from 1945–1953) probably pulled more pranks in the White House than any other president. One of his efforts scared the pants off a reporter. Truman was planning a trip to South America. Several newspaper reporters were going with him. Often when people traveled to South America, they had to get painful shots to protect them from yellow fever. One of the reporters, Tony Vaccaro, was terrified of needles. He was overjoyed when he found out he didn't have to get the shot. Then, suddenly, he was told that the president had decided he *did* need to get the shot. A terrified Vaccaro was dragged to the White House clinic. He was told to lie down on a couch, facing the wall, with his pants down. (Yellow fever shots were given in the rear end, not the arm.) Seconds later, Vaccaro heard the door open and a familiar voice said, "This won't hurt you a bit, Tony." He turned around to see President Truman holding a gigantic hypodermic needle, the kind used by veterinarians on horses. Vaccaro started to scream. Then he saw that the president was smiling, and realized it was all a joke.

All aboard! Lyndon B. Johnson takes some guests for a ride.

LYNDON B. JOHNSON

Lyndon B. Johnson (president from 1963–1969) loved cars and kept a large collection of them at his Texas ranch. One of his most unusual cars was an Amphicar—it looked like a normal car, but it worked like a boat if you drove it into the water. Johnson realized this vehicle was perfect for pranking guests. He would invite his visitors to take a drive around the ranch with him in the blue convertible. When they got to a steep hill at the edge of a lake, Johnson would let the car pick up speed. Then he would start to yell, "The brakes don't work! The brakes won't hold! We're going in!" As the car entered the lake, the passengers would panic—until they realized they were in an Amphicar. Instead of sinking, they were motoring across the lake. Later Johnson would tease his visitors for trying to save their own skins instead of the president.

GEORGE H. W. BUSH

Presidents shake a *lot* of hands, but only George H. W. Bush (president from 1989–1993) is known to have taken advantage of this excellent pranking opportunity. He sometimes hid a small metal disk known as a joy buzzer in his palm and surprised high-powered politicians with a vibrating handshake. He also spent his first day in the White House tricking everyone with a squirting calculator. Somehow, he found time to run the country, too.

George H. W. Bush

BARACK OBAMA

Thousands of people got to hear a president make a prank phone call in 2009. Virginia governor Tim Kaine was nearing the end of his term. He was in the middle of hosting his last radio call-in show, called "Ask the Governor," when a call came in from a man saying he was "Barry from D.C." The man said he wanted to ask about traffic in Virginia. Kaine was poised to take the question when the caller said something much more interesting: He revealed that he wasn't just any old Barry from D.C.— he was President Barack Obama (first elected president in 2008) from the White House. For a second, Kaine was speechless. Then he broke into laughter and was visibly moved. He later learned that the radio station had arranged the call as a humorous— and memorable—sendoff. It's not every day that you get fooled by the nation's Prankster-in-Chief.

Barack Obama

I vote for more pranks!

QUIRKY QUARTER

Prank #50

DIFFICULTY LEVEL: EASY

FIRST, SPREAD THE GLUE AROUND EVENLY.

PRESS DOWN ON IT FOR A WHILE. MAKE SURE IT'S REALLY STUCK TO THE SIDEWALK.

JACK SHOULD BE BY ANY SECOND...

HRRRRRGGGGRRRRRR...

WOW, GRAVITY IS REALLY STRONG THIS MONTH!

the prank

It's always nice to find a quarter on the sidewalk—except when you can't get it *off* the sidewalk, no matter how hard you try. This simple prank has a quick payoff, worth at least 25 cents.

what you need

* A quarter
* White glue (Elmer's or a similar brand)

what you do

THE SETUP

1 Squeeze a little bit of glue onto the back of the quarter and spread it with your finger so the surface is evenly coated.

2 Place the quarter on the sidewalk or other pavement where you know your victim will see it. Press down hard for a minute until it sticks. Make sure it will have a few minutes to dry before your victim arrives.

PULL THE PRANK

1 Wait for your victim to walk up, see the coin, and say something like "Wow, this is my lucky day."

2 When the person tries to pick up the coin and can't, act really baffled. "Wow, I heard the earth's gravitational pull is unusually strong this month. I bet that's why it's stuck."

3 If you need your quarter back, you can use water to dissolve the glue.

VERY IMPORTANT PRANKS
V.I.P.

Funny Money

An anonymous prankster in Spain must have gotten tired of looking at the face of King Juan Carlos on his country's euro coins. He used his impressive art skills to transform the royal face into the bald-headed king of cartoon comedy, Homer Simpson. The coin found its way to a candy store in the north of Spain, where the owner discovered it while counting up the day's earnings. Thousands of fans of *The Simpsons* have offered to buy the kooky coin, but the store owner seems to want to keep Homer at home.

The work of a true (prank) artist.

RESTAURANT EXTRA·SPECIAL SPECIALS

DIFFICULTY LEVEL: EASY

I ACT NORMAL WHEN THE MENU ARRIVES.

MENUS, LADIES...

THANK YOU!

I SLIP ON MY OWN "SPECIAL" SPECIALS!

TODAY'S SPECIALS

OH MY GOSH! THAT GUY LOOKS JUST LIKE JUSTIN BIEBER!!

WHERE?

ALL OF A SUDDEN, I'M NOT VERY HUNGRY ANYMORE.

the prank

Eating out at restaurants is usually fun. But it's not always *funny*. You can fix that. See how long it takes your victim to realize that today's specials are especially weird.

what you need

* "Today's Specials" menu on page 207
* Scissors
* A paper clip

what you do

THE SETUP

1 Carefully cut out the list of specials on page 207.

2 The next time you go to a restaurant, bring the list and a paper clip with you (hide them in your pocket or a bag).

PULL THE PRANK

1 Sit next to your chosen victim. As soon as the menus arrive, secretly attach the fake specials list to the front of your menu with the paper clip (or slip the list into the menu's plastic sleeve).

2 When your victim isn't looking, quickly switch your menu with hers. If you need to distract your victim, you can say something like, "Wow, can you believe what that lady over there is wearing?" and point to a far corner.

3 Once you've made the switch, go back to studying your menu and wait for your victim to notice the unusual specials. If the person comments about the dishes being strange, say, "You should order one so we can all try it!"

VERY IMPORTANT PRANKS
V.I.P.

The Left-Handed Burger

A fast-food restaurant pulled a fast one on April Fools' Day 1998. Burger King ran a full-page ad in USA Today announcing the introduction of a Left-Handed Whopper, a burger designed just for left-handed people. The ad explained that even the special sauce had been "rotated 180 degrees." Thousands of people went to Burger King to order the new burger, not realizing it was a King-size joke.

RESTAURANT MISFORTUNE COOKIES

DIFFICULTY LEVEL: EASY

OH BOY, FORTUNE COOKIES!

NO ONE'S LOOKING, I'LL JUST GRAB MY PRANK MESSAGE...

THE CHEF SNEEZED IN Y

WOW, BRO. MAYBE YOU SHOULD OPEN ANOTHER COOKIE.

the prank

One of the best things about eating at a Chinese restaurant is opening the fortune cookie at the end of the meal and finding out what your future holds. You can make this experience even better by messing with the messages.

what you need

* Fortune cookie messages on page 189
* Scissors

what you do

THE SETUP

1 Carefully cut out the fortunes on page 189 and put them in your pocket the next time you go to a Chinese restaurant.

On the fortune slips:
- The chef sneezed in your food. ☺
- The waiter secretly hates you. ☺
- Trust me, you do not want to know your fortune. ☺
- All our fortune tellers are busy. We apologize for any inconvenience. ☺
- Would you mind leaving? We need this table. ☺

PULL THE PRANK

1 When the fortune cookies arrive, sneak a fake fortune out of your pocket. Here are a couple of ways you can use it—or you can come up with your own ideas:

* Open your own cookie and say, "Wow! You guys are not going to *believe* what mine says!" Then pass the fake fortune around the table.

* Ask someone if you can open his or her cookie. (Offer to let the person have your cookie so they don't get suspicious.) Hide a fake fortune in the palm of your hand. As you open your victim's cookie, switch the real fortune for the fake one. Read it silently to yourself, and then say, "Um, you got a kind of weird one" and hand it to your victim.

SHAMPOO SHENANIGANS

DIFFICULTY LEVEL: EASY

I'LL UNSCREW THE LID...

I'LL COVER THE OPENING WITH PLASTIC WRAP...

I'LL MAKE SURE NO EXCESS PLASTIC IS SHOWING

NOW, I'LL TEST IT, TO MAKE SURE NOTHING IS COMING OUT...

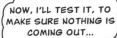

?

the prank

Long, hot showers are good for relaxing and forgetting your troubles—until you reach for the shampoo and can't get it to come out of the bottle. This prank is guaranteed to put an abrupt end to any joyful singing that's coming from the shower.

what you need

* A bottle of shampoo or conditioner with a top that screws on and a little spout that you pull up or press down to open
* Plastic wrap
* Scissors

what you do

THE SETUP

1 Carefully cut a small piece of plastic wrap, just a little bigger than the bottle opening (about an inch and a half across).

2 Unscrew the cap on the bottle of shampoo. Place the piece of plastic wrap over the bottle opening. Carefully screw the cap back on.

3 Test the prank. Open the spout and try squeezing some shampoo onto your hand. Nothing should come out. If shampoo *does* come out, you may need to use a bigger piece of plastic wrap.

PULL THE PRANK

1 Leave the shampoo bottle in the usual place in the shower and wait for someone to try washing his or her hair.

2 If your family keeps multiple bottles of shampoo and conditioner in the shower, rig every single bottle for an even better effect.

SNOT THAT'S NOT

Pranks #54-56

DIFFICULTY LEVEL: *EXPERT*

HERE COMES MANNY. LET'S PRANK HIM...I'LL LOAD A BIG GOB OF FAKE SNOT IN THIS TISSUE...

HEY MANNY...AH, **AH-CHOO!**

GESUNDHE

WOW, MUST BE SOMETHING WRONG WITH ME... LOOK HOW MUCH SNOT I JUST BLEW OUT!

the pranks

Your hardworking nose and sinuses produce about a quart of snot every day! That may sound disgusting, but the slimy stuff actually does a very important job: Mucus in your nose traps germs and dust you breathe in, preventing the stuff from getting into your lungs, where it could cause an infection. *Fake* snot, on the other hand, has only one purpose: gross pranks. And it's *snot* hard to make.

what you need

* Measuring cups
* Water
* A small bowl
* A tablespoon
* Unflavored gelatin (look for it in the baking section of your supermarket)

* A fork
* Corn syrup (also in the baking section)
* Paper towels
* Red food coloring
* A few strands of cooked spaghetti

#54 Basic Snot: what you do

THE SETUP

1 **Ask an adult** to help you boil some water and pour ½ cup of it into the bowl.

2 Carefully sprinkle in 2 tablespoons of gelatin so it evenly covers the whole surface.

3 Let the gelatin soften for a few minutes. Then use a fork to gently push any undissolved gelatin into the water so it gets soaked, and stir the mixture with the fork.

4 Stir in ¼ cup corn syrup.

5 Let the mixture thicken for about 1 hour. The longer you wait, the more solid it will become. It's up to you how runny you want your snot to be. If it gets too thick, you can add water, a little bit at a time, to make it runnier.

PULL THE PRANK

1 Put a big gob of the fake snot in a paper towel and hold it in your hand with the snot hidden.

2 When your victim is nearby, sneeze loudly into the paper towel and then pretend to blow your nose into it. You can make a good nose-blowing sound by voicing the letter *K* in the back of your throat. (Practice this beforehand.)

3 After "blowing" your nose for a long time, stop and look into the open paper towel and act horrified. You can say, "Eww! Look how much snot I just blew

out." Show the huge blob of mucus to your victim and enjoy the reaction of disgust.

4 You can also try leaving a glob of fake snot in the sink or next to a box of tissues in the bathroom, or putting some on your face and pretending you don't realize it's there. Or invent your own uses.

#55 Bloody Snot: what you do

THE SETUP

1 Follow the basic snot recipe on page 137. Add 3 drops of red food coloring, and you'll have bloody snot.

PULL THE PRANK

1 Follow steps 1 through 3 of "Pull the Prank" from page 137 for regular fake snot.

2 When you get to step 3, you can scream when you look inside the paper towel. Then tell your victim that your doctor warned you not to blow your nose too hard or your brains might start coming out of your nose. Or say that you have a spider living in your nostril and it keeps giving you a bloody nose.

GEEZ, MY DOCTOR WARNED ME NOT TO BLOW TOO HARD, OR MY BRAINS MIGHT COME OUT!

UGGH! THAT'S DISGUSTING!

#56 Worm in the Nose: what you do

ADULT HELP

THE SETUP

1 Make basic snot using the recipe on page 137.

2 Put a piece of cooked spaghetti in a blob of fake snot. Leave one end of the noodle sticking out slightly.

PULL THE PRANK

1 Place the blob of snot in your left hand (you can put it inside a paper towel if you want).

2 When your victim is nearby, sneeze and then pretend to blow your nose as described on page 137. But hold both hands together as you blow.

3 While "blowing," grab the end of the noodle with your right hand, place it inside your nostril, and press the fingers of your right hand against the outside of your nose to hold the noodle in place. Keep your nose close to the blob so your victim cannot see you position the noodle.

4 With your right hand holding your nose, slowly raise your head. The noodle will gradually get pulled out of the blob. You should watch it in horror and then scream and say something like, "Oh my God, there's a worm in my nose! Help!"

SPACE CADET

DIFFICULTY LEVEL: EASY

I MADE IT THROUGH THE FIRST ROUND, I THINK THEY WANT TO INTERVIEW ME NEXT WEEK...HERE'S THE OFFICIAL LETTER!

the prank

Russia sent the first dog into orbit in 1957, and since then, men, women, cats, monkeys, and even spiders have gone into space. Kids, however, have been left out of the action—until now. Convince your friends and family that the United States is preparing to send the first child into space, and the lucky junior astronaut just might be you!

what you need
* "First Child In Space Acceptance Letter" on page 225
* Scissors

what you do

THE SETUP

1 Carefully cut out the "First Child In Space Acceptance Letter" on page 225.

PULL THE PRANK

1 You can pull this prank on friends, siblings, or your parents. Start by asking if they have heard about the First Child In Space program. When they say no, tell them that you learned about it from your science teacher and it's really cool.

2 Then say, with a hint of pride in your voice, "I already sent in my application, and guess what? I got through the first round and now they're going to interview me!" Then show them the "official" letter and fact sheet.

* If you're pranking friends or siblings, tell them they better hurry up and apply if they want a chance at this out-of-this-world opportunity.

* If you're pranking your parents, say you need their permission to continue your application. If they balk, explain that it's a great learning opportunity, not to mention that you will be famous for the rest of your life.

Sports Pranks

Professional athletes are lucky: They get to play games for a living. But they are also under a lot of pressure. That might explain why they pull so many pranks—it helps lighten things up. Here are eight winning sports pranks. It's no accident that four of them involve baseball. Baseball players are definitely the champs when it comes to pranks.

let the games begin!

HE TOOK EVERYONE FOR A RIDE

At the 1904 Olympic Games in St. Louis, Missouri, American marathon runner Fred Lorz started getting muscle cramps. He managed to run nine miles before giving up and jumping into a race official's car. He rode the next 11 miles. Then, as a joke, he got out and ran the rest of the way, entering the stadium and crossing the finish line before anyone else. The crowd cheered like crazy, not realizing it was a prank. President Franklin D. Roosevelt's daughter even placed an honorary wreath on his head before Lorz admitted he'd pulled a fast one. He went on to win the Boston Marathon the following year—without hitching a ride.

A BAD TRADE

Pitcher Brett Myers deserves a Most Valuable Prankster award for the perfect stunt he pulled on teammate Kyle Kendrick when they were both playing for the Philadelphia Phillies. One day in 2008, the manager of the Phillies (who was in on the prank) called Kendrick into his office and told him that he was being traded to a Japanese team for a player named Kobayashi. Myers arranged for a local TV news team to be there to film the announcement—and Kendrick's shocked reaction. The poor guy was so stunned he couldn't speak for most of the news conference. He apparently forgot that American and Japanese teams never trade players. Myers went to incredible lengths to pull off the hoax, getting the local TV station involved and even having Kendrick sign fake trade papers. Luckily, Kendrick learned it was all a prank before boarding a plane to Japan.

SOMETHING FISHY

Moe Drabowsky was a good pitcher, but he's remembered more for his pranks than for his game. He loved to hide snakes—both fake and real—in other players' lockers. He would also use the phone in the bullpen, where pitchers warm up, to order Chinese food during a game. In 1969 Drabowsky and a couple of his Baltimore Orioles teammates, Eddie Watt and Pete Richert, snuck into the opposing team's bullpen, slipped four live goldfish into the water cooler, and scurried out. The fish seemed unbothered, but the bullpen manager was furious. Either he had no sense of humor—or he was very thirsty.

FLAMING UNDIES

Before the Summer Olympic Games begin, runners carry a torch from Greece, where the ancient Games started, to the host country. In 1956 the torch had a difficult journey to Melbourne, Australia. It got drenched in torrential rains and went out several times. At one point, it was so hot that the runners nearly collapsed. But nothing beats what happened when the torch arrived in the city of Sydney, Australia. A champion runner named Harry Dillon was scheduled to carry the torch into the city and present it to the mayor, Pat Hills. About 30,000 people lined the streets, waiting for Dillon to arrive. At last, a runner came sprinting into the city. The crowd cheered as he made his way to the mayor and handed over the torch. The mayor prepared to start his speech when someone whispered in his ear, "That's not the torch." The mayor looked down and realized that the "torch" he was holding was a wooden chair leg with a can on top. Inside the can was a pair of underwear soaked in kerosene to make it burn like the Olympic flame.

The mayor took the prank in good humor, and minutes later the official torchbearer arrived. The Olympic-sized prank was the work of a college student named Barry Larkin and eight of his friends. When Larkin returned to college, his fellow students gave him a standing ovation. Even the head of the college could appreciate a prank well done: "Good job, son," he said.

Sid Finch: The amazing pitcher who never was.

THE BEST PITCHER WHO NEVER EXISTED

In 1985 *Sports Illustrated* magazine asked the writer George Plimpton to write an article about April Fools' jokes in sports. When Plimpton complained that most of the pranks he found didn't translate well into print, his editor suggested he pull his own prank. The resulting story was one of the best sports hoaxes of all time.

Plimpton invented a young pitcher named Sidd Finch who he said was training with the New York Mets. According to Plimpton's article, Finch could throw a fastball at the mind-boggling speed of 168 miles per hour. His unusual background and eccentric habits made him stand out, too: Finch had learned how to throw a baseball in a monastery in Tibet, and he liked to pitch while wearing just one hiking boot.

When the story appeared on April 1, 1985, many readers fell for it—and so did a few baseball pros. Two major league managers called the commissioner of baseball to complain that it would be unsafe for hitters to stand at the plate when Finch unleashed his fastball.

DUDE, WHERE'S MY CAR?

One spring day in 2008, as the Chicago Cubs were beginning practice, third baseman Aramis Ramírez walked over to a coach named Tim Buss and asked him what his car was doing up on a ramp next to the bullpen. Buss looked up and saw a wrecked 1995 Nissan: The body was dented and all the windows were smashed. "That's not my car," said Buss. Then he did a double take: "Dude," he said, "that *is* my car!" He knew the Cubs pitching staff was famous for its pranks, but this time he thought they had gone too far. It was his wife's car, and now he had to tell her it was destroyed. The pitchers all kept a straight face throughout the practice. Later, pitcher Ryan Dempster told him to stop pouting and come "see something." He brought Buss to where a brand-new SUV was waiting for him. Buss was nearly moved to tears. "They're great guys," he said. And great pranksters, he might have added.

THE THRILL OF VICTORY

French prankster Rémi Gaillard has been pulling daring stunts in public and posting them online since 1999. In 2002 Gaillard fooled French TV reporters and the president of France into thinking he had helped win an important soccer tournament called the Coupe de France. Dressed in the uniform of Lorient, the winning team, he ran onto the field at the end of the match. Jumping up and down, he celebrated with the rest of the team, shook hands with President Jacques Chirac, and even signed autographs without anyone realizing that he wasn't on the team.

FOUL PLAY

After WNBA star Diana Taurasi was named to the 2012 U.S. Olympic women's basketball team, she pulled a prank on her Phoenix Mercury teammates worthy of a gold medal. Taurasi and three teammates were doing a video interview for a local sports news website. The interviewer asked Taurasi if it was true that an Olympic rule prevented her from playing with the Mercury until after the Olympics. Taurasi got very angry and stormed off the set. Seconds later, she stormed back and explained to the interviewer that her teammates did not know about the rule, and she had been planning to break the news herself.

Meanwhile, Taurasi's three teammates did not look good. Their faces were frozen in shock and anger at the news that they would be playing without their star. About a minute later, though, they came back to life when Taurasi smiled and said, "You just got punk'd." Player Nakia Sanford leaped out of her seat and started pounding Taurasi—playfully, of course. It turns out Taurasi had teamed up with the interviewer and invented the story about the Olympic rule. Based on that performance, Taurasi might want to consider an acting career after basketball.

the prank

Everyday objects like drinking straws often make excellent materials for pranks. With a little practice, you can use a straw to magically transform a glass of apple juice into soda and leave your victims thinking they are losing their minds!

what you need

* 2 drinking glasses
* 2 different colored beverages
* 2 plastic drinking straws (*not* the see-through kind)

what you do

THE SETUP

1 Offer your friend or sibling a choice of the two beverages, making sure each drink looks and tastes very different from each other. For example, one drink could be cola, and the other apple juice.

2 Prepare the drinks where your victim can't see you. Fill your victim's glass almost to the top with whatever she asks for. This is drink #1. Now fill another glass about three-quarters full with the other beverage. This is drink #2.

3 Place a straw in drink #2 and let it touch the bottom of the glass. Put your index finger over the top of the straw so it's completely covered. This will keep the liquid inside the straw.

4 Carefully remove the straw from the glass, keeping your index finger over the opening, and put it in drink #1. Don't remove your finger until the straw is touching the bottom of the glass.

5 Now put the second, clean straw in beverage #2. That's your drink.

PULL THE PRANK

1 Serve the drinks. Your victim will be shocked when she takes the first sip and the drink doesn't taste a bit like what she asked for. You can add to the confusion by saying, "So what does it taste like?" When she says it tastes like beverage #2, say, "But it doesn't even *look* like it. Maybe because you are looking at my drink, your brain cells got mixed up and that's what you're tasting!"

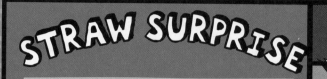

STRAW SURPRISE IN A RESTAURANT

Prank #59

DIFFICULTY LEVEL: EASY

GET SOME KETCHUP PACKETS...

PUT IT IN HER SODA.

HURG ERGH...

THIS SODA IS GREAT, HOW IS YOURS?

the prank

Most people use the little ketchup packets at restaurants to add some tomato flavor to their hamburger or fries. Tasty, but not much fun. The real appeal of ketchup packets is that they fit nicely on the end of a straw—which means you can use them to add tomato zest to your victim's soda. Perform this sneaky switcheroo when eating out with your family or friends.

what you need

* A drink with a straw in a paper or plastic cup (*not* the see-through kind)
* A ketchup packet
* A straw

what you do

THE SETUP

1 When you order your food, ask for ketchup packets, or grab some from the counter.

2 Choose someone in your party who has a drink with a straw in it to be your victim. The drink should be in a paper or plastic cup that you can't see through.

3 Wait for the person to go to the bathroom or come up with another way to get her away from her drink for a minute. You can ask her to go get you some more napkins, for instance.

PULL THE PRANK

1 When your victim is gone, tear open one end of the ketchup packet. Remove the straw from her drink, stick one end in the ketchup packet, and put the whole thing back in the drink with the packet at the bottom.

2 When your victim complains that there is something wrong with her soda, say something innocent like, "Weird. What's wrong with it? Mine is totally fine!"

3 Be prepared to buy your victim a replacement drink!

STRAW TROUBLE

Prank #60

DIFFICULTY LEVEL: EASY

FIRST, I POKE ONE HOLE IN EACH STRAW.

WHO WANTS DRINKS?

UHHHHHHGGH...

the prank

With the prick of a pushpin, turn a plastic straw into the world's most frustrating beverage utensil and leave your victims wondering if they've forgotten how to drink properly.

what you need

* A pushpin
* Plastic drinking straws

what you do

THE SETUP

1 Use the pushpin to poke a tiny hole near the top of each straw. Be careful not to push it all the way through to the other side of the straw. You just want one hole, not two.

PULL THE PRANK

1 At mealtime or snack time, serve everyone drinks with trick straws in them. (Give yourself a regular straw, of course.) No matter how hard your victims try, they won't be able to suck the liquid through the straw.

2 As you merrily slurp up your drink say, "Wow, you guys don't seem to have much lung power. You should try exercising more."

the prank

Maybe you've heard of "Take Your Daughters and Sons to Work Day." Fool your parents into thinking that your school is holding a "Take Your Teacher Home Day" and watch them panic.

what you need

* "Take Your Teacher Home Day" letter on page 209
* Scissors

what you do

THE SETUP

1 Carefully cut out the "Take Your Teacher Home Day" letter on page 209. (You can also photocopy or scan it at a larger size if you want it to look even more authentic or print one out at workman.com/pranklopedia.)

PULL THE PRANK

1 Wait until you have your parent's full attention—when he or she asks you what happened in school is the perfect time. Take out the letter and give it to your parent. Explain that the letter describes a new program your school is participating in, and your teacher said to make sure your parents read it.

2 If your parent starts asking questions, just say you only know what it says on the paper. Then, sit back and watch the freak-out.

Prank #62

DIFFICULTY LEVEL: EASY

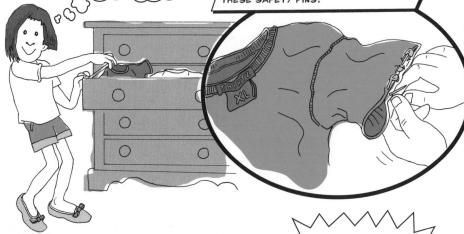

the prank

Sewing shut the arms of someone's shirt is an old—and very effective—prank. This modern version is easier because you use safety pins instead of a needle and thread.

what you need

* Safety pins (about 10 small- or medium-size pins)

what you do

THE SETUP

1 Sneak into your sibling's or parents' bedroom when they're not around. Remove a clean T-shirt from the bureau or wherever they keep them.

2 Turn the T-shirt inside out. Taking care not to poke yourself, use the safety pins to pin closed the edges of both sleeves.

3 Now turn the shirt right side out and smooth out the sleeves. You shouldn't be able to see the safety pins.

PULL THE PRANK

1 Carefully fold the shirt and put it back where you found it. The next morning when your victim is getting dressed, listen for any unusual sounds. If things suddenly become very quiet, it could mean the person gave up and went back to bed.

2 This prank also works on long pants or underpants (boxer shorts are preferable). Follow the preceding steps, pinning the legs closed instead of the sleeves. If you're lucky, you'll be around to watch your victim hopping around on one leg, trying to get the other leg through the closed hole.

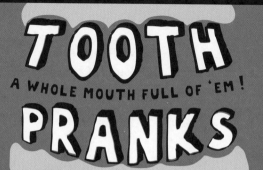

the pranks

They don't say it on the package, but uncooked pizza dough is perfect for making false teeth—or creating the illusion of missing teeth. You'll find tubes of pizza dough in the refrigerated section of the supermarket. You only need a little bit to make fake teeth, so this prank comes with a bonus: pizza for dinner!

what you need

* A tube of uncooked pizza dough
* A plate
* Flour
* A mirror
* Red, green, and blue food coloring
* A plastic cup or an empty plastic container (like a yogurt container) that you can throw away
* Baking soda (for getting the food coloring off your fingers)

Tooth Preparation

First, fix the dough so it's a little less sticky. Break off a small amount—about 1 teaspoonful—and put it on the plate. Add a tiny bit of flour and mix it in with your fingers. Then decide what kind of teeth you want to make and follow the directions.

#63 Buck Teeth: what you do

THE SETUP

1 Pinch off 2 small pieces of prepared dough about the size of your front teeth. Use your fingers to mold each lump so it's shaped like a tooth, only longer. It helps to look at your own teeth in the mirror as you do this.

2 While looking in the mirror, press the fake teeth onto your two front teeth. The dough should stick to your teeth. (If it is *too* sticky and won't leave your fingers, add more flour.) Use your fingers to shape your new teeth so they look just like your own teeth only bigger.

continues

PULL THE PRANK

1 Go up to your victim and say that your dentist tried a new kind of braces, but they didn't work right. They made your front teeth stick out, and now you have to go back next week to see if they can be fixed. Or you can say nothing, and just act like your teeth are completely normal.

#64 Black Teeth: what you do

THE SETUP

1 Put one drop each of red, blue, and green food coloring in the plastic cup. Together, they'll make black.

2 Dip a small lump of floured dough in the food coloring. Use your fingers to mix it in so the dough looks black. (Your fingers will turn black, too, but don't worry—it isn't permanent!)

3 Break off a tooth-size piece of the black dough and, while looking in the mirror, press it onto one of your front teeth. Use your fingers to mold the dough so it covers your tooth completely but isn't too thick. You might need to start over with a smaller piece. The idea is to black out one tooth so it looks like it's missing.

4 Before you pull the prank, use baking soda and water to wash the food coloring off your fingers.

PULL THE PRANK

1 Walk up to your victim and act totally normal. Wait for the person to say, "Yikes, what happened to your tooth?" Explain that you ate so much candy that your tooth fell out during the night. Or say that when you bit into a piece of bread in the school cafeteria, it was so stale and hard that your tooth popped out. Or make up your own version of the *tooth*.

CHOOSE YOUR FAVORITE EXPLANATION!

I ATE SO MUCH CANDY LAST NIGHT, MY TOOTH CAME OUT.

I JUST WOKE UP THIS MORNING AND IT WAS GONE . . .

THE BREAD AT SCHOOL LUNCH WAS SO HARD, MY TOOTH BROKE OFF!

GUESS I BRUSHED TOO HARD THIS MORNING.

WHAT HAPPENED?

#65 Bloody Teeth: what you do

THE SETUP

1 Follow steps 1 and 2 for making a black tooth, but use two or three drops of red food coloring *only*.

2 Break off a tooth-size piece of the bloody dough. Press it onto a front tooth. Be sure to do this while looking in the mirror to make sure it looks real. You want it to look like you just had a tooth pulled.

PULL THE PRANK

1 Hold your hand up to your mouth and moan a little as you walk up to your victim. Or put a little bit of red food coloring on a paper towel so it looks like blood, and hold the towel up to your mouth as you approach. Say that you had a really bad toothache and your friend had to yank your tooth out with pliers. Or explain that you were at a baseball game and were trying to catch a ball but forgot to put your hands up and your tooth got knocked out. Then move your hand or the paper towel away from your mouth and say, "How does it look?"

2 For extra drama, when you pull the prank, put a second slightly bloody "tooth" in the paper towel. Approach your victim while holding the paper towel up to your mouth and say that your tooth almost got knocked out and is now hanging on by a thread. Pretend to move your front tooth around with your fingers and the paper towel, keeping your mouth mostly closed. Then quickly pull the paper towel down, keeping your mouth closed, and look inside the towel while gasping. Say, "Oh, gross, that last thread just broke" and show your victim the tooth inside the towel.

WHAT DID YOU DO?

MAKE UP A GOOD STORY.

AH... THAT FEELS BETTER!

NOW, IF I CAN JUST STOP THE BLEEDING...

GET READY, TOOTH FAIRY!

I THINK I'LL BECOME A DENTIST.

GROSS.

TV Pranks

O **ften, the best** part about pulling a prank is watching the victim's reaction. Television producer Allen Funt understood that when he created the pioneering show *Candid Camera* in the 1940s. Since then, countless other prank shows have lit up the little screen. Tune in for some highlights.

Candid Camera hosts Alan Funt and Bess Myerson.

THE INVISIBLE CAMERA!

The show *Candid Camera* introduced a formula that is now familiar: A hidden camera catches ordinary people responding to weird and funny situations. In an episode that aired in the 1960s, a car that had had its engine removed pulled into a gas station. (The "driver" actually coasted the car down a slight hill.) After gassing up, the driver complained to the attendant that the car wouldn't start. When the worker lifted the hood to check the engine, he was astonished to find that it was missing. Later, he learned that he had been pranked when he heard the show's famous catchphrase, "Smile, you're on *Candid Camera*." *Candid Camera* aired, in various formats, for about 50 years. It paved the way for other American prank shows, including *Totally Hidden Video* and *Just for Laughs*. The *Candid Camera* concept spread around the world, with Britain, Germany, Japan, and other countries producing their own shows.

CELEBRITY SILLIES

In the 1980s celebrities got in on the act when the show *TV's Bloopers & Practical Jokes* started doing pranks on famous people. Actor Ashton Kutcher took the idea further in 2003 with his show *Punk'd*. In the first episode, singer Justin Timberlake was fooled into thinking that government agents were seizing his home because of unpaid taxes. He was sweating until he heard the show's catchphrase, "You just got punk'd!"

TALK-SHOW TRICKS

Talk-show hosts often use pranks to spice up their programs. In the 1990s David Letterman used to go on location and pose as a worker at fast-food drive-throughs. Ellen DeGeneres is known for pranking her guests by having a staffer sneak up behind them during the show and scare the living daylights out of them. Late-night host Jimmy Kimmel gets parents to prank their kids and send in the videos—occasionally he turns the tables and has kids trick their parents.

A NEW TWIST ON AN OLD IDEA

Audiences seem to have an endless appetite for watching pranks in action. More recent shows include *Impractical Jokers*, where four comedians challenge each other to pull pranks on strangers without knowing ahead of time what the prank will be. In *Betty White's Off Their Rockers*, comedian Betty White sends feisty senior citizens into the streets and malls to play practical jokes on the younger generation.

YOUR TURN

Today you don't have to be famous for your pranks to be seen by millions of people, thanks to YouTube. A search for "pranks" turns up not only videos of old *Candid Camera* and *Punk'd* episodes but also videos made by regular people. Of course, not everyone has Allen Funt's talent for setting up the perfect prank, and some are funnier than others.

the prank

Umbrellas are good protection from rain but not from pranks. Fill a family member's umbrella with confetti or cereal and the next time it rains, your victim will experience a special shower.

what you need

* Your victim's umbrella
* Confetti, or something that works like confetti, such as dry oatmeal or plain cereal

what you do

THE SETUP

1 Open the umbrella and turn it upside down so the tip is resting on the floor.

2 Put a few handfuls of the confetti or cereal inside. Then carefully close the umbrella and fasten it shut. Clean up any spilled confetti or cereal.

PULL THE PRANK

1 Put the umbrella back where you found it. The next time it rains, keep an eye out to see if your victim grabs the umbrella. If possible, follow your victim out the door so you can witness the effects of the rare weather pattern.

VERY IMPORTANT PRANKS

V.I.P.

The Umbrella Fella

Brian G. Hughes was a wealthy New York banker famous for pulling practical jokes that poked fun at people who were greedy or who thought they were very important. One of Hughes's favorite pranks was to leave expensive umbrellas in public places. When someone took one and opened it up, their little crime became public—a sign dropped down that said: "Stolen from Brian G. Hughes." Hughes probably would have been happy to know that when he died in 1924, his obituary described him as a famous practical joker first and a banker second.

VOMIT!

DIFFICULTY LEVEL: EXPERT

LOOKING GROSS ALREADY!

I WAIT FOR IT TO DRY COMPLETELY SO IT WON'T STAIN ANYTHING.

IT WASN'T ME!

MOM, RALPH LEFT US A SOGGY GIFT ON THE BACKSEAT...

the prank

Fake vomit has a longer life than almost any other prank. You can use it again and again: on car trips, your sister's bed, your aunt's couch . . . the only limit is your imagination (and the patience of your friends and family). Instead of spending money on plastic vomit, make your own fake vomit at home. It takes a little time, but it's totally worth it.

what you need

ADULT HELP

* Measuring cup
* Water
* A small bowl
* A box of lemon gelatin mix (Jell-O or similar brand)
* A spoon
* A jar of applesauce (chunky style is best)
* A microwave-safe bowl or small saucepan
* A tablespoon
* A packet of unflavored gelatin (look for it in the baking section at the store)
* A teaspoon
* Uncooked oatmeal
* Cheddar cheese or similar hard cheese (optional)
* A plate
* A spatula

what you do

THE SETUP

1 **Ask an adult** to help you boil 1 cup of water and pour it into a bowl. Pour in the packet of lemon gelatin mix and stir well. Add 1 cup of cold water and stir again.

2 Put ¼ cup of applesauce in the microwave-safe bowl. Stir in 2 tablespoons of the lemon gelatin liquid.

3 **Ask an adult** to help you heat the applesauce mixture in the microwave for about 30 seconds, until it's hot but not boiling. (If you don't have a microwave, ask an adult to help you heat the applesauce in a pan on the stovetop over low heat, stirring occasionally. When it's hot, get help emptying it into the bowl.)

continues

vomit!
(continued)

4 While the applesauce is still hot, sprinkle the packet of unflavored gelatin on top and stir well.

5 Sprinkle in a teaspoon of oatmeal. If you want, crumble a small piece of cheese into the mixture.

6 Pour the barf mixture onto a plate. It should be liquid enough to spread out. Use a spoon to move the solid chunky part around so it looks like real vomit. You might want to sprinkle a little more oatmeal or cheese on top.

7 Put the plate of puke in a safe place to cool and harden. It needs at least 4 hours.

8 When the vomit is dry, use the spatula to remove it from the plate. Make sure it is completely dry so it won't stain anything when you use it.

PULL THE PRANK

1 The world is full of opportunities to use your fake vomit. Here are just a few ideas:

❋ *Car trip:* During the ride, place the fake vomit on the floor of the backseat. Then start complaining about feeling sick to your stomach. Say things like, "I'm not feeling too well," "I'm a little nauseated," or "I really hope I don't throw up." Then cough lightly and make some retching sounds. Wait in

silence for a few seconds, and then in a small voice, announce that you just puked on the floor. Or, if your dog is along for the ride, put the vomit on the backseat and say, "Uh-oh, I think Ralph got carsick when we weren't looking."

❋ *Movie theater:* Place the vomit on the floor next to your friend's feet when he isn't looking. Then point to it and say, "Ew. Looks like someone ate too much popcorn."

❋ *Late to the bathroom:* Leave the vomit on the floor next to the toilet for someone to find.

❋ *A sick night:* Put a piece of fake puke in your sibling's bed before bedtime, or place it on the floor for her to find when she wakes up in the morning.

❋ *Use your imagination!* Carry a piece of fake vomit wherever you go, and keep an eye out for interesting places to leave it. But do not bother bringing it to school—unless, of course, it is "Bring Some Fake Vomit to School Day."

Horace de Vere cole:

Always Horsing Around

Horace de Vere cole was born into a wealthy family in Ireland in 1881. He started doing pranks in college and never stopped. One of his tricks was to challenge a well-known politician to race him down a London street for fun. Cole would let the fellow pull ahead of him and then yell, "Stop, thief!" until a police officer showed up. The prank went a little too far when a member of Parliament got arrested as a pickpocket. Hopefully, the guy had a good sense of humor.

Cole seemed unable to resist the urge to pull a prank. He even pranked the citizens of Venice, Italy, when he was there on his honeymoon. Venice is a low-lying city filled with canals instead of roads, and when Cole was there, the city had no horses—which is what gave Cole his idea for a prank. In the middle of the night, he went to the mainland and returned with a boatload of horse manure. He scattered it around the city's most famous square, the Piazza San Marco. The next morning, Venetians were scratching their heads trying to figure out how their horseless city had produced all that manure.

An artist's interpretation of the manure-filled square.

167

WATER YOU STANDING THERE FOR?

DIFFICULTY LEVEL: MEDIUM

GREAT. NOW YOU TRY!

HEY! WAIT, WHERE ARE YOU GOING?

OOPS!! I FORGOT SOMETHING

the prank

Horace de Vere Cole was an Irish poet born in 1881 who seemed to spend as much time creating pranks as he did poems. (You can read more about Cole on page 167.) In one of his pranks, Cole pretended to be a surveyor—a person who measures land in preparation for building. In those days, surveyors used string to take measurements. Cole would ask a passing stranger to help him out by holding one end of the string. Then he would go around the corner and ask another stranger to hold the other end of the string. At this point Cole would depart, leaving the two men holding the string. In this prank you walk away leaving your victim in a similarly silly situation.

what you need

* Two rimless plastic cups
* Water

what you do

THE SETUP

1 Fill each cup about halfway with water.

PULL THE PRANK

1 Walk up to your victim carrying the two cups of water. This prank works best indoors so that your victim won't just dump the water on the ground. Explain that you want to see if you can balance two cups of water on your hands and you need some help.

2 Give your victim the cups of water and hold your hands out in front of you, *palms down*. Ask your friend to balance one cup on each of your hands. This might take a little while. You will have to work together to find the best place to put the cups, but don't give up. It's definitely possible.

3 Once both cups are balanced, say, "Awesome!" and ask your friend to remove them. Then say, "Now, let's see if you can do it."

4 Repeat the process, this time balancing the cups on your friend's hands. Remember, his palms must be facing *down*. When the cups are perfectly balanced, walk away. You can pretend you have to go check on something or just leave without saying a thing. Your friend is left standing there, with no way to remove the cups from his hands without dumping the water.

X-TRA-TERRESTRIAL VISITORS

DIFFICULTY LEVEL: *EXPERT*

WOW, THE WEIRDEST THING HAPPENED TO ME LAST NIGHT...

WHY, WHAT HAPPENED?

IT'S THE EXACT SAME MARK I SAW ON THE ALIEN'S HEAD! IT WASN'T A DREAM!

WO

WHERE ARE THE ALIENS?

WHAT IS HE TALKING ABOUT AND WHAT IS HE WEARING ON HIS HEAD??

NICE!!

the prank

The chances that extraterrestrial beings will land on Earth are pretty slim. But the idea makes great material for a science-fiction movie—or a prank. With a little paint and a lot of fast talking, you can dupe a younger sibling or gullible friend into thinking that an alien visited you in the middle of the night and left a mysterious mark on you. And now, the alien would like to meet your friend . . .

what you need

* Face paint or nontoxic washable paint
* A plastic cup
* Newspaper or paper towel
* A cotton ball or clean sponge
* Scissors

what you do

THE SETUP

1 To create the mysterious mark left on your arm by the alien, first choose the color paint you want to use to create the mark. You can use a single color, or mix several colors together in the plastic cup to create a color that makes you think of aliens.

2 Put newspapers or a paper towel down on the table to protect it from the paint.

3 Place the arm to be painted on the newspaper or paper towel. Keep the palm of your hand facing up.

4 Decide what you want your alien mark to look like. It's best to make a simple shape.

5 Dip your finger (or a cotton ball or piece of sponge) in the paint and carefully draw the symbol on your forearm. Apply a very thin coat of paint—you want it to look like part of your own skin.

6 Wait for the paint to dry.

PULL THE PRANK

1 First thing in the morning is a good time to pull the prank, and younger siblings are the best targets.

2 This prank requires some top-notch acting, so think through what you are going to say beforehand and rehearse the story when you are alone.

continues

X-Tra-terrestrial Visitors

(Just make sure you are out of earshot of your family or they will think you have lost your mind.)

3 Your story can go something like this, but be prepared to improvise and answer any questions that your victim asks:

✳ Start by describing what a strange night you had. Say something like: "The weirdest thing happened to me last night. It was so bizarre, I can hardly believe it myself." Pause and take a deep breath, as if you are upset.

✳ Your victim will probably ask, "What? What happened?"

✳ Continue your story, speaking in a slightly shaky voice: "I was sound asleep when I felt something brush across my arm and it woke me up. At first I couldn't see anything. Then I noticed that some kind of creature was in the room. It definitely wasn't a human—it was short with a huge head that had a weird mark on it. I was about to scream when the thing started talking in this really strange voice—like a cross between a human and a computer. It said, 'Hello, [your name]. We've been hoping to establish communication with you. Please don't be alarmed. We are curious about your planet and how you live. We thought you might be able to help us.'"

✳ Keep going with the story: "I said, 'Why me? And who are you?'" The creature said it came from a planet called Malarka in another galaxy and they picked me because I was born on

[your birthday], which according to them is a sign that we will work together well. Then it said it had to go but it would attempt to communicate with me again today through a magnetic system. It said I should wait at [choose a location] today at [choose a time] and that I should bring you because you seem like somebody who can be trusted."

✳ Now comes the part where you use the mark on your arm as proof that an alien really visited you. Say: "I fell back to sleep, and when I woke up this morning, I figured it was all a dream. But then I saw this." Hold out your arm so your victim can see the mark and say: "It's the exact same symbol I saw on the alien's head! When it brushed my arm, it must have marked me. So it wasn't a dream!"

✳ Now it's time to get your sibling or friend to take action: "I want you to come with me today when the alien returns. You don't have to be afraid. There was nothing scary about it. But we have to wear metal on our heads so their magnetic messages will get through. Meet me at [choose a location] at [choose a time] and cover your head with a pot lid or a big piece of foil. And don't be late. This is really an amazing opportunity to communicate with extraterrestrial creatures!"

✳ Make sure some friends or family members will be present at the time and place you picked. When your victim shows up with a pot lid or foil on his head, act like you have no idea why and just shake your head in amazement if he starts talking about aliens.

X-TRA-TERRESTRIAL X-TRAS

To make the alien visit more convincing to your victim, you can leave "evidence" in different places where he will see it. For example:

1 Create the alien mark in the grass near your house, using nontoxic paint. Or use a shovel to create the shape in dirt or gravel.

2 Make the alien mark appear on a piece of toast at breakfast. Here's how:

✳ Mix together 7 drops of red food coloring, 4 drops of yellow, and 2 drops of green to make brown.

✳ Dip the handle tip of a plastic spoon or fork in the food coloring and use it to draw the alien mark on a piece of bread.

✳ Toast the bread and place it on the table where your victim will see it.

3 Follow the instructions in the Message from a Ghost prank on page 81 to make the alien mark appear in the bathroom mirror.

4 Use your imagination to think of other places where the aliens can leave their mark!

X-tra-terrestrial Files

D **oes intelligent life** exist beyond the planet Earth? No one knows for sure. But so far, the only "evidence" has turned out to be extraterrestrial pranks like these.

Aliens like pranks, too!

MOON CREATURES

In 1835 a New York newspaper announced the discovery of life on the moon. According to the paper, a famous British scientist had invented a powerful new telescope that allowed him to view the surface of the moon. Every day for a week, the newspaper ran a story describing the astonishing creatures that lived on the moon: lunar bison; fire-emitting, two-legged beavers; and "man-bats"—humanlike creatures with bat wings. The paper even printed pictures of the strange creatures. Newspapers across the country reprinted the articles, and soon it was all people could talk about. Eventually they realized they had been fooled, even though the newspaper never 'fessed up to the hoax. For years after, people used the phrase *moon hoax* for any story that sounded like it was made up.

An 1835 print shows lunar man-bats.

SIGNS OF PLANT LIFE IN OUTER SPACE?

Sometimes pranksters have to wait a long time for their joke to be discovered. But 100 years? That's how long it took scientists to realize that a meteor that landed in southern France was evidence of a sense of humor—not extraterrestrial life. On May 14, 1864, a meteor shower fell near the town of Orgueil. Someone collected samples of the meteorites and sent them to the natural history museum in a nearby city. Museum workers sent most of the samples to other museums but kept two in a sealed glass jar. They soon forgot about them.

Then, a century later, in the early 1960s, researchers opened the jars and studied the samples. They were shocked at what they found: Buried deep inside the meteorites were plant seeds—evidence that life must exist somewhere in outer space, wherever the meteorites came from! On closer look, the scientists discovered that the seeds were actually from France—someone had apparently mixed them with ground charcoal, stuck them inside the soft space rock, then sealed the outside with glue. Unfortunately, the prankster who went to all that trouble wasn't alive to enjoy the prank.

THE "WAR OF THE WORLDS" HOAX: WHAT REALLY HAPPENED?

The War of the Worlds radio broadcast is probably the most famous extraterrestrial hoax in history. Orson Welles was a famous movie director—and perhaps the most famous prankster who never was. On October 30, 1938, on his weekly radio show, he broadcast a play based on a story by H. G. Wells called "War of the Worlds." Welles announced at the start of the broadcast that what listeners were about to hear was a play. But some people missed that part or ignored it. As the play progressed, listeners heard what sounded like series of terrifying "news" announcements.

First there was a report that astronomers had detected blue flames on the surface of Mars. Minutes later, an announcer reported that a meteor had just landed on a field near Grovers Mill, New Jersey. Then another report: It wasn't a meteor but a spaceship-shaped object—and a creature with tentacles was climbing out of it. The creature was wearing a huge, metal contraption and it was starting to march across New Jersey, blasting earthlings with heat rays and toxic gas.

The story goes that hundreds of people living near the site jumped in their cars and started to flee. The truth is probably not nearly as exciting. While some people may have believed the story, many more listeners reported that they simply felt disturbed or frightened by the play. There is little evidence of the mass panic that newspapers later reported. Neither phone lines nor highways were jammed. In fact, the real hoax could be that people believed the newspaper reports of "mass panic." What really happened that night is that millions of people sat at home listening to a really good, really scary science-fiction story.

UNIDENTIFIED FLYING REINDEER

In December 1965 the manned space shuttle *Gemini 6* was orbiting Earth when NASA's Mission Control received a startling message from astronauts Wally Schirra and Thomas Stafford. The two reported seeing an unidentified flying object traveling north to south. They said it consisted of one command module with eight smaller modules in front and that the pilot of the command module was wearing a red suit. The folks at Mission Control were mystified—and a little alarmed—until they heard the sound of "Jingle Bells" being played on the harmonica and sleigh bells. Schirra and Stafford had sneaked the instruments onboard and decided to play an out-of-this-world Christmas prank.

One of the largest crop circles ever found.

A NEW CROP OF HOAXES

One of the longest-running extraterrestrial hoaxes in history started in the late 1970s when a weird "sign" appeared in a field in England. Stalks of corn had been flattened to the ground to form a huge, perfect circle. A few years later, more circles appeared in a wheat field, and this time reporters rushed to the scene, followed by hundreds of tourists. Everyone wanted to know what had produced the mysterious pattern. Was it air currents? Was it crazed animals running in a circle during mating season? Or was it a prankster—and if so, why were there no footprints or other signs of human involvement? Maybe it was a landing site for an alien spaceship?

Over the next decade, hundreds of other crop circles appeared in fields, mostly in England, but also in other parts of the world. People known as "cerealogists" became obsessed with the circles. Most believed they were coded messages left by creatures from another planet. In 1991, two creatures from Earth named Doug Bower and Dave Chorley confessed that they had created most of the crop circles as a hoax. They wanted to fool people into thinking that UFOs (Unidentified Flying Objects) had landed on Earth. Their method was simple: They used wooden planks and a string to flatten crops at night when no one could see them. What about the circles that the two pranksters did *not* make? Chances are that copycat pranksters created them—although no one knows for sure.

ALIEN FROM THIS PLANET?

On March 31, 1989, motorists in West Sussex County, England, were astonished to see a giant, saucer-shaped spaceship land in a field. Some were so frightened they drove to a phone to call the police. When the police arrived and started walking toward the glowing vehicle, a door opened in the bottom of the craft and a little alien in a silver spacesuit stepped out. The officer closest to the "alien" ship took one look and ran away. It turned out there was nothing to fear. The tiny alien was a man hired by Richard Branson, the billionaire owner of Virgin Atlantic airline. Branson, who loved pranks and hot-air ballooning, had engineered the stunt for April Fools' Day. He had had a hot-air balloon built to look like an alien spaceship. His original plan was to land in a park in London, but the wind blew him down in the field a day early.

Richard Branson with his daughter and the "spaceship."

177

YUCKY SANDWICH

DIFFICULTY LEVEL: **EXPERT**

YUK! "MOLDY" CHEESE!

"FURRY" BREAD!

GROSS!

YOU'VE GOT TO TRY THIS!

the prank

Take this disgusting-looking old sandwich to school and fool your friends into thinking you've lost your mind by calmly biting into it. Or serve it to yourself at home during a family lunch.

> **WARNING**
> THIS PRANK SANDWICH IS PERFECTLY SAFE, BUT REAL MOLD CAN MAKE YOU VERY ILL. SO NEVER, EVER EAT ANYTHING THAT HAS REAL MOLD ON IT.

what you need

* 2 slices of American cheese (orange-colored)
* Flour
* A small dish
* 1 tablespoon peanut butter
  (use hummus if you are allergic to peanuts)
* 1 variety package of food coloring
* 2 small bowls
* 1 dull knife
* 2 slices of bread
* 1 teaspoon powdered sugar

what you do

THE SETUP

1 The first step is to "age" the slices of cheese. Put a small amount of flour in a dish. Dip your finger in the flour and dab it on the edges of the cheese so it looks like spots of mold.

2 Now create some "moldy" bread. Put the peanut butter and 4 drops of blue food coloring in a bowl and mix them together with the knife. The mixture should turn green.

3 Use the knife to lightly dab green peanut butter on top of one slice of bread in moldlike patches. Don't overdo it—a light touch makes the mold look more realistic. Then sprinkle a little powdered sugar on some patches. Turn the bread over and tap it with your finger to shake off the excess sugar. You want just enough to give the mold a furry appearance.

4 In the second bowl, mix together two drops of each color of food coloring.

Dab this mixture on or next to the green areas of the bread to make black blotches.

5 Now assemble the sandwich using the other slice of bread and the cheese. Make sure the cheese slices are sticking out so you can see the mold.

PULL THE PRANK

1 Wrap the sandwich in plastic and take it to school. Or serve the sandwich to yourself on a plate at home when you're lunching with your family.

2 Before you take the first bite, say something like, "Mmmm, this is my new favorite sandwich!" Then eat the way you normally do, as if there is nothing unusual about your lunch. When people say things like, "Gross, your sandwich has mold on it!" just smile and say, "You gotta try this!" and offer the person a bite.

ZZZ... SHORT SHEETS

Prank #71

DIFFICULTY LEVEL: MEDIUM

I'LL FLIP THE SHEET SO THE END USUALLY AT THE TOP OF THE BED IS AT THE BOTTOM.

NOW I FOLD UP THE BOTTOM EDGE TO THE TOP OF THE BED SO THE SHEET IS FOLDED IN THE MIDDLE.

I'LL PUT BACK THE BLANKET AND PILLOWS AND TUCK IN ALL THE EDGES.

GAH!

SLEEP TIGHT, ALEX!

the prank

Short-sheeting a bed is one of the oldest pranks in the book. Keep the ancient bedtime tradition alive by pulling this prank at sleepovers, on your siblings, or on your parents.

what you need

✳ The sheets and bed of an unsuspecting friend or family member

what you do

THE SETUP

1 To do this prank, you need to remake your victim's bed, so wait until she is out of the house.

2 Take off the bedspread, blanket, pillows, and top sheet.

3 Spread the top sheet on the bed so the end that usually goes at the top is at the bottom. If there's a fancy border, it should face *up*. Make sure there is plenty of sheet sticking out at the top and tuck that part under the mattress.

4 Now fold the top sheet almost in half by bringing the bottom edge up toward the top, so it's even with the edge of the mattress. Put the blanket on and fold the top edge of the sheet over it. If there is a fancy border, it should show.

5 Tuck in all the edges of the sheet and blanket. Make sure the sheet is pulled tight.

6 Now put the pillows and bedspread back where they belong.

PULL THE PRANK

1 When your victim gets into bed and tries to stretch out her legs, she won't be able to. Her feet will get stuck in the folded sheet.

2 If you get accused of any wrong-doing, say, "You must have been really tired when you made your bed this morning. It's crazy what you did with the sheets!"

the prank

If you've already short-sheeted every bed in the house—at least twice—try this bed prank. Your family will start checking under the sheets every night before getting in bed.

what you need

* Small balloons (6 to 10 of them)
* Water
* A towel or paper towels

what you do

THE SETUP

1 Run the water in the sink until it's very cold. Then use the cold water to make 6 to 10 *small* water balloons. To make a water balloon, fit the opening of the balloon over the faucet. Slowly turn on the water. When the balloon is just filled, but not stretched out, turn off the water. Remove the balloon and tie a knot in the opening.

2 Use a towel or paper towel to dry off the balloons. Make sure no water is leaking from them. If you want to make them colder, leave them in the fridge for a few hours before pulling the prank.

PULL THE PRANK

1 Sneak into your victim's bedroom. Pull back the blankets and sheet and place the cold water balloons in the middle of the bed so the person's feet will touch them when he gets into bed.

2 Now put the sheet and blanket back just the way you found them. If you made the water balloons small enough, they won't show under the blankets. When your victim gets into bed, the balloons will feel like some creepy, cold-blooded creature that has invaded the bed.

AFTER Z

Did you pull every prank from A to Zzz? That's a lot of pranks—but it's only the beginning of your career as a prankster. Often the best pranks are the ones you invent yourself, using everyday materials. Keep your eyes, ears, and mind open to pranking opportunities. As the dedicated prankster Hugh Troy (see page 35) once said, "You will make life more interesting for yourself—and for other people."

P.S. How many times did YOU get punked while reading this book? Though a master prankster such as yourself probably catches onto a hoax as quickly as a Whoopee Cushion toots . . . here's the official list of pranks that your faithful author planted in these pages for your enjoyment.

1 **PAGE 9: THE PRANKSTER HALL OF FAME: ANIMALS PULL PRANKS, TOO!** While it's amazing to picture wild hyenas pranking each other with homemade whoopee cushions, unfortunately, no one has ever witnessed such a thing. Dr. Sheila Getchew is a made-up scientist. Did she *getchew* to believe her fake research?

2 **PAGE 37: COMPUTER PRANKS AT WORKMAN.COM/COMPUTERPRANKS.** Those additional computer pranks were pranks on *you*, but you didn't fall for them, did you? Instead, you sent friends to the fake website and they are busy enjoying their subscriptions to the Cottage Cheese of the Month Club!

3 **PAGE 93: THE PRANKSTER HALL OF FAME: INTELLIGENCE TEST: DO PRANKS MAKE PEOPLE SMARTER?** Dr. Fran Luschinsky and her discoveries about the effects of pranks on the brain are completely made up. But don't worry if you spent some time pacing around your living room with a pineapple on your head while repeating the word *knarp* (which, by the way, is *prank* spelled backward). It can be a very therapeutic exercise—at least for those around you, who will enjoy all the health benefits of hysterical laughter.

The Goods

Ready-to-use labels, letters, signs, and more!

Tape this sign above the toilet.

THIS TOILET IS VOICE-ACTIVATED. SAY "FLUSH TOILET" IN A LOUD, CLEAR VOICE WHEN YOU ARE DONE USING IT.

Tape this sign to the bathroom door.

RESTROOM CLOSED FOR MAINTENANCE

PLEASE USE THE OUTDOOR FACILITIES UNTIL FURTHER NOTICE

Prank #8: Bathroom Signs p.22
Tape this sign to the bathroom mirror.

OBJECTS IN MIRROR ARE
WEIRDER THAN THEY APPEAR

Prank #52: Restaurant Misfortune Cookies p.132
Pretend you found these misfortunes in fortune cookies.

☺ Your lucky number is
1466732290668. ☺

☺ You should have ordered
the chicken. ☺

☺ The person at the next table is
planning to steal your wallet. ☺

☺ This piece of paper
contains no MSG. ☺

☺ Do not remove from cookie
under penalty of law. ☺

☺ You just harmed an
innocent cookie. ☺

☺ Small misteaks leaf a bad
impression. ☺

☺ All our fortune tellers are busy. We
apologize for any inconvenience. ☺

☺ The waiter secretly hates you. ☺

☺ Trust me, you do not want
to know your fortune. ☺

☺ Help! I have been kidnapped
and forced to bake cookies. ☺

☺ You will get new glasses very soon. ☺

☺ He who breaks cookie will get
broken heart. ☺

☺ You will be very successful
as long as you don't

☺ The chef sneezed in your food. ☺

☺ Machine wash warm; tumble
dry. Do not dry clean. ☺

☺ You smell weird. ☺

☺ Would you mind leaving?
We need this table. ☺

HONK IF YOU HATE CAR HORNS

DON'T LIKE OUR DRIVING?

YOU SHOULD SEE US DANCE

DO NOT TAILGATE

BUMPER CONTAINS

EXTREMELY POWERFUL MAGNET

BABY RATTLESNAKE ON BOARD

Tape or hold this sign up to a car window or tape it to the bumper

Proud owner of an OBNOXIOUS BUMPER STICKER Collection

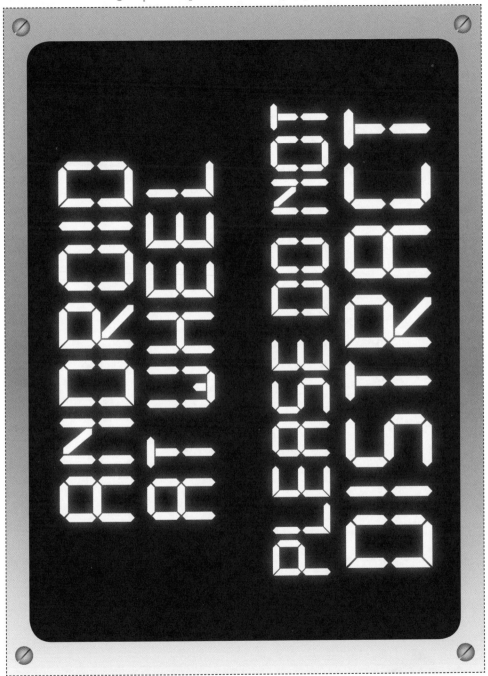

Name _____ Date _____

Math Homework

Answer each question. Be sure to show how you solved each problem.

) Josh has 5 mini pizzas to share with 4 friends. Two pizzas have mushrooms, 2 have pepperoni, and 1 is plain. Jasmine only eats plain pizza. Zach won't eat mushrooms or onions. Carly and Owen will eat pepperoni and mushrooms, but no onions. Josh will eat any kind of pizza. If Josh cuts each mini pizza in half, how should he divide up the halves so each person gets 2 halves each? How much pizza will be left over?

) Ryan gets allowance money every day. On Monday he gets 5 cents. On Tuesday he gets 12 cents. On Wednesday he gets 19 cents. On Thursday he gets 30 cents. On Friday he gets 35 cents. How much will he get on Saturday? How much will he have by the 12th day? The 16th day? When will he be able to buy a new bicycle?

) Will's family is planning a summer car trip. They have 2 weeks to drive from Los Angeles to New York. Along the way they will stop for 2 days in Duluth, Minnesota, to visit Aunt Nina and for 1 day in Pittsburgh, Pennsylvania, to see Uncle Hubert. The mom and dad will each drive half of each day. Dad drives at 55 mph and Mom drives at 65 mph. If they make 4 rest stops of 20 minutes each every day plus a 30-minute lunch break, how long will the whole trip take? You can use a map to help you solve the problem.

) Emma was 3 feet tall when she was 4 years old. She was 4 feet, 1 inch when she was 8 years old. At age 10 she was 4 feet, 8 inches tall. At age 15 she was 5 feet, 3 inches. How old will she be when she is 5 feet, 7 inches tall?

) John's hair grows half an inch every 2 weeks. He got his hair cut on November 19. The barber took off 1 inch and John's hair was 4 inches long when he was done. On December 19 he went back to the barber and had another half inch cut off. He wants to get 1 inch cut off at his next haircut, and he wants his hair to end up being 5 inches long. When should he go to the barber next?

----

k your parents for help with these impossible math problems.

TODAY'S SPECIALS

Appetizers

Cream of Milk Soup
Garden Salad with Soil-Encrusted Croutons
Smoked Salmonella

Entrées

Freely Deranged Chicken on a Bed of Tired Spinach
Grilled Catfish with Steamed Hairballs
Veggie Burger with Bacon and Sausage Topping
Hamster Steak with Rash Potatoes
Steamed Muscles in Garlic Barbelle Sauce

Desserts

Leftover Cheesecake with Fresh Fruit Topping
Chocolate Moose

* All our food is prepared to order and served on real plates.
* Please add a dollar to your bill if you take a toothpick or mint on the way out.
* A 15% gratuity is automatically included for parties that are really obnoxious.

TYTHF
Take Your Teacher Home Foundation

Dear Parent:

Your child's school is participating in a new national program called "Take Your Teacher Home Day." The program is designed to allow teachers to get to know their students' families and the home environment better. Your child's teacher will come to your house on a prearranged evening and stay for four to five hours. Please make sure your house is clean. Prepare your usual dinner, but make sure you have enough for one extra mouth. The meal should have at least three courses. Teachers with special dietary needs will inform you of them in advance.

After dinner, your child's teacher will follow you around the house, observing everything you do and asking questions. Feel free to organize some fun activities for the teacher to do with the rest of the family, anything from playing charades to baking cookies together!

We will send more information and a list of dates when your child's teacher is available in a few months. We hope you will enjoy participating in this innovative program!

Sincerely,

Joe King

Joe King
Executive Director
Take Your Teacher Home Foundation

---

nk #61: Take Your Teacher Home! p.152
d this letter to a parent or guardian.

Prank #6: Bad Breath p.18

Tape or glue this label around a roll of candy and offer one to a friend!

Prank #40: Loony Labels p.100

Tape or glue these bursts to household products.

Tape or glue this label onto a tin of mints.

Prank #42: Lucky Lottery Ticket p.104

Cut out this lottery ticket and pretend you just won the prize.

Put this inside your sibling's or parent's favorite box of cereal.

NAME _____

STREET _____

CITY   STATE   ZIP

BLOOD TYPE

$1

- All prizes must be claimed within 90 days. Ticket purchaser must be at least 21 years of age; ticket holder must be at least 7 years of age or at least 2 feet tall. On average, approximate odds of winning are the same as the odds of being elected president.

- Prizes of $1,000 or more must be claimed at a Lottery Office. A $500 fee will be charged for excessive gloating at the counter.

- In addition to cash prizes, winners will receive an all-expenses-paid trip to Transylvania where they enjoy a private dinner with Count Dracula and a week-long stay at the country's top school for young vampires-in-training. Fang implants and complimentary blood smoothies included.

9 780 61 16 556

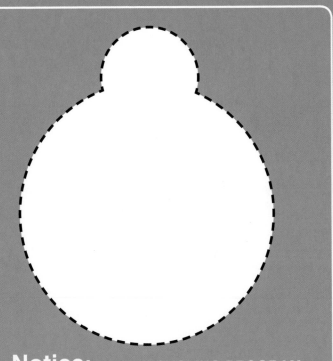

Prank #17:
Doorknob
Hangers
p.46

Hang this on
the door of your
house for your
parents to find.

Notice: NEW RECYCLING PROGRAM

Dear Resident:

Your household has been selected for a pilot test of a
new recycling program.

Beginning next month, you must separate the following
items from your garbage:

- ☑ **bones (chicken, fish, meat)**
- ☑ **used tissues**
- ☑ **eggshells**
- ☑ **items that are moldly (cheese, fruit, etc.)**
- ☑ **cat litter (remove all solid matter first)**

You will receive more details about the program in the
coming weeks. **Participation is mandatory.** Your garbage
will be inspected, and failure to comply will result in fines.

THANK YOU FOR YOUR COOPERATION!

(workman)

Prank #17:
Doorknob
Hangers
p.46

Hang this on
the door of your
house for your
parents to find.

ATTENTION

SEWER LINE REPAIR

As part of our infrastructure improvement program, sewer lines in your area will be flushed out and repaired on **THURSDAY** of this week.

Please follow these precautions:

- **Do not use toilets** between the hours of 7:00 A.M. and 5:00 P.M.

- **Keep toilet lids closed** all day to avoid sewage backup and odor problems.

We apologize for any inconvenience.

(workman)

Prank #38: Kitchen cabinet caper p.96

Tape or glue this label on a 6-ounce can.

The food your dog really wants!

Sneaky Snacks
Dog Food

...and rawhide.

NET WT. 6 OZ.
DOG FOOD

Fortified with vitamins, minerals,

Perfect for puppies!

#1 with BAD DOGS

Delicious morsels of sneakers, socks, grass, bones, and table scraps in beef-flavored gravy.

INGREDIENTS:
Finely chopped sneakers, socks, grass, bones, chew toys, table scraps, upholstery. Also contains water, beef flavoring, rawhide, homework, and vegetable oil.

Guaranteed to satisfy all your dog's chewing and mischief needs. Dogs who eat Sneaky Snacks are 70% less likely to destroy furniture.

FUN 2 CHEW

DIST. BY SNEAKY SNACKS INC., Petaluma, CA

workman

ank #38: Kitchen
binet caper p.96
pe or glue these labels
6-ounce cans.

Crampy's

COLORFUL SOUPS THAT DRESS UP YOUR DINNER TABLE

Rainbow **in a Bowl**

Cream of Pink

A SUBTLE BLEND OF RED AND WHITE
PIGMENT IN CREAMY BROTH

SOUP

NET WT.
6 OZ.

MIX SOUP WITH ONE CAN OF MILK

For a deeper pink, use less milk.
Heat in microwave or on stovetop.

Try other Rainbow in a Bowl soups:
- Cream of Purple
- Classic Beige
- Chunky Teal

Questions, comments?
Call 555-RAIN-BOW

(workman)

Nutrition Facts	
Serving Size ½ cup	Servings 2.5
Calories	65
Amount Per Serving	% Daily Value
Total Fat 0.6g	.008%
Saturated Fat 0.3g	50%
Pastel Fat 0.3g	50%
Sodium 2mg	5%
Vitamin P	1%
Pigment Iron 0.5g	10%
Tint 9mg	95%

* Percent Daily Values are based on a 2,000-color diet.

R O Y G B I V

(workman)

NATURE'S FINEST SOUPS

WILD FOWL CLASSICS

★ SPARROW ★

*A tender piece of
sparrow in every bite!*

NET WT. 6 OZ.

NATURE'S FINEST SOUPS

✓ Low Fat
✓ Excellent Source of Songbird
✓ Pigeon-Free

READY TO EAT. (REMOVE NEST
BEFORE SERVING.)
HEAT IN MICROWAVE OR ON STOVETOP.
YOU'LL HEAR A CHIRP WHEN IT'S READY!

Visit our website for fun edible
birdhouse serving ideas!
www.fowlfun.net
Questions, comments?
Call 555-FUN-FOWL

Nutrition Facts	
Serving Size 1/8 cup	Servings 20
Amount Per Serving	
Calories 2	Calories from Fat .00003
	% Daily Value*
Total Fat .06g	22%
Wing Fat 0.5g	41%
Tail Fat 6.4g	
Cholesterol 22g	41%
Sodium 40mg	23%
Total Carbohydrate 3g	15%
Flyber 6g	11%
Sugars 0	
Avian Protein 17g	
Vitamin Beak 1%	Irony 110%
Clawcium 3%	Twig 95%

* Percent Daily Values are based on eating
like a bird.

INGREDIENTS: WATER, CREAM, SALT, SPARROW,
MODIFIED CLAW, GROUND BIRDSEED, ESSENCE OF
CHIRP, NATURAL SWEETENERS, BROWN #1, GRAY
#3. MAY CONTAIN TRACES OF TWIG.

DIST. BY NATURE'S FINEST SOUPS,
FOWLER, IL USA

(workman)

50395
9 WING IT

Presidential Pet Achievement Award

This certificate recognizes the contributions of _____ to the emotional

health and general welfare of the _____ household and the nation

at large. This pet has demonstrated exceptional intelligence, cuteness,

loyalty, and/or cuddliness above and beyond the call of duty.

Peter Pettingill

Peter Pettingill, *Chairman*
President's Council on Pets

workman

National Space Exploration Agency
Washington, D.C.

Dear Applicant:

Thank you for your interest in the First Child In Space (FCIS) program. We have received your initial application, and it has been approved. Congratulations!

In three to four weeks, we will contact you to arrange to interview you and your parent or guardian at our Washington, D.C., offices. At that time, we will also administer tests to measure your ability in math, science, and other subjects.

Please see the reverse for more information about the FCIS program. We look forward to meeting you.

Sincerely,

James Chapin

James Chapin, Director
NSEA First Child In Space Program

National Space Exploration Agency

FIRST CHILD IN SPACE PROGRAM

Have you ever dreamed of orbiting the Earth on board a space shuttle? Your dream could become a reality! To celebrate 30 years of manned space shuttle flights and mark the end of the shuttle program, the National Space Exploration Agency (NSEA) will send the first child into space next year. If you are between the ages of 7 and 15, physically fit, with aptitude in math and science, you are eligible to apply. Ten children will be selected to participate in a one-year training program. Upon completion of the program, one participant will be chosen to become the first child in space.

THE FCIS TRAINING PROGRAM

The First Child In Space (FCIS) Training Program will take place in Cape Canaveral, Florida. Housing and meals will be provided for the child and one parent or guardian.

The Training Program will include:

- rigorous fitness classes to prepare for the physical demands of space travel
- weekly flight simulations
- a minimum of 20 hours in a microgravity environment, with instruction in how to eat, sleep, exercise, bathe, and use the bathroom in space
- courses in basic astronomy, physics, aerospace engineering, and the history of space travel, taught by NSEA instructors. (Certified classroom teachers will provide instruction in regular academic subjects to ensure that trainees do not fall behind in school.)
- lunches and dinners with active and retired astronauts
- training in public speaking

THE FLIGHT

The trainee selected to be the First Child In Space (FCIS) will join a crew of four astronauts aboard a recently refurbished space shuttle that will orbit the Earth for approximately five days. The dates of the mission will be announced closer to the launch. The FCIS will be a passenger on the shuttle, not an active crewmember, but he or she will be required to assist with meal preparation and cleanup and write a daily blog about the experience of traveling in space. Upon return to Cape Canaveral, the FCIS must be available for TV and other media appearances. The FCIS will also be asked to speak at schools across the country over the course of the next year.

TO LEARN MORE: Visit fcis.not.

(workman)